the leaves are falling in rainbows

Science Activities for Early Childhood

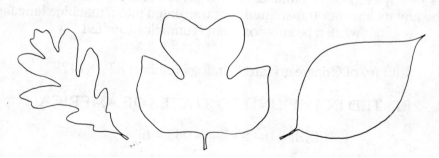

Michael E. Knight, Ph.D.
Early Childhood Department
Kean College of New Jersey

Terry L. Graham, M.A. Early Childhood
Early Childhood Consultant
Atlanta, Georgia

Humanics Limited * Atlanta, Georgia

HUMANICS LIMITED
P.O. Box 7447
Atlanta, Georgia 30309

Library of Congress Card Catalog Number: 83 - 81429

PRINTED IN THE UNITED STATES OF AMERICA

ISBN: 0 – 89334 – 045 – 6

"What Is It?" from *Air All Around* by Tillie S. Pine and Joseph Levine. Copyright 1960 by Tillie S. Pine and Joseph Levine, McGraw Hill, Publishers. Reprinted with permission.

"First Snow" from *A Pocketful of Rhymes* (1957) by Marie Louise Allen. Copyright 1939 by Harper & Row, Publishers, Inc. By permission of the publisher.

"You Light Up My Life" from the book, *Teaching Children To Love Themselves* by Michael E. Knight, Terry Lynne Graham, Rose A. Juliano, Susan Robichaud Miksza and Pamela G. Tonnies 1982 by Prentice-Hall, Inc. Published by Prentice-Hall, Inc., Englewood Cliffs, NJ 07632

Dedication

To Laura,
who loved her rainbows.

Table of Contents

Introduction

Science is a daily experience for young children. Children come to school with a wealth of information that can be channeled into scientific investigations. A science curriculum should grow out of the children's daily experiences. In the past, science was "taught" by abstract methods, with text books and through lectures. These methods provide very little, if any, real learning for children. Young children must learn through firsthand experiences.

The teacher's role is to create an atmosphere where children are free to explore a large variety of materials. A good teacher listens to and observes children. He or she is genuinely concerned for the child's self-image. In a safe and secure setting, the children are encouraged to discover the world around them. The teacher establishes a "need to know."

Build on the interests of the children when providing science experiences. A science lesson is often stimulated by the questions of the children themselves. Respond to what they bring to school. The teacher helps the child by assisting, directing, and inquiring. Your questions can lead children to their own answers.

When selecting materials and activities, be aware of these science processes:

investigating	discovering
observing	fostering thinking skills
defining	finding solutions
comparing	relating
grouping	sorting

classifying

Activities that incorporate these processes help the child get to know about the physical world.

The activities should:

1) incorporate active learning;
2) allow the teacher to employ inquiry strategies that focus on discrepancies and on the actions in the situation;
3) help the child focus on *transformations* – on change from one state to another – rather than on the beginning and final status, and
4) involve problems where rate of change is rapid and observable, such as water changing color or ice melting.

It is important that children develop a scientific attitude and a questioning mind. Help children delight in the process of discovery by not telling them all they need to know. Help them to observe all aspects of things before reaching conclusions and to understand that conclusions are not absolute. Children need to develop minds that can adapt to change and accept mistakes; new questions and discoveries come from mistakes.

The activities presented in this book focus on the child as a "natural explorer." Active exploration is the way that children get to know the physical attributes of objects, how they function, and what can be done with them. Even young children can identify problems, observe discrepancies, draw inferences, generate hypotheses, interpret results, and draw conclusions. The Piagetian approach encourages active exploration of objects through manipulation and transformation. The children have a controlled environment with teacher assistance, but are allowed a great deal of freedom. Class discussions help stimulate abstract thinking. The motivation to learn comes from the children themselves, and they acquire knowledge about their physical world for its own sake.

The title of this book was given by a four-year-old girl in my preschool class. When Adrian commented that "leaves were falling in rainbows" in her yard, I was overwhelmed by the beauty of her language and the deep thought it implied. It inspired this book with hope that many teachers will be inspired by the children they teach and that all will strive to open new worlds for children through science exploration and discovery.

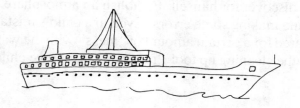

Chapter One

W · A · T · E · R
Play

Water holds a natural attraction for most three and four-year-old children. It is inexpensive and, if presented in an interesting way, can be a great learning center. The children can actively explore and discover many concepts on their own, with guidance and encouragement from the teacher. Water is easy to work with and provides the child with a pleasant tactile experience. It does what the child wants it to; therefore, the child feels successful when he works with water. Experiences with water are relaxing and often offer the emotionally upset child a comforting activity.

Young children enjoy stirring, mixing, heaping, digging, filling, emptying, sifting, splashing and pumping water. Water can be used for representation and role-play — making coffee, cakes and lemonade, floating boats and making bridges.

The water area can be arranged in a variety of ways to make the best use of available space. A water table built of wood and lined with metal or plastic works well, and there are many such tables available commercially. When space does not permit a table, substitute a baby bathtub or dish pans. A child's small wading pool also offers possibilities for both sand and water play.

Water play is delightful outdoors when the weather is warm. When the weather is cold, explore the properties of snow and ice. Bring pans of snow inside to the water area and let children create with it as they would with sand. When the snow melts, what will it look like if we refreeze it? Let's try!

Water play is a daily experience for the preschool. It is not an isolated activity and should be incorporated into the daily routine. The experiences in this unit can add greatly to the child's development when he is allowed to experiment, explore and discover for himself. Piaget would tell us that children can only learn when they are actively involved with objects and materials and are able to act spontaneously. Keep the materials in your water area new and interesting. Don't interrupt a child's thinking but do ask questions that will cause him to think, predict and observe. Be a guide, not a lecturer. Refrain from telling a child something he can discover for himself. Establish an atmosphere that encourages trying, asking questions, and making some errors. Even in a child's mistakes there is a degree of correctness. Be prepared for a certain amount of "mess" with the water area, but remember, there is learning in the cleaning up too! Praise and encourage children's discoveries.

Discovering & Exploring Water

SETTING UP A "WATER DEPARTMENT"

EQUIPMENT:

measuring cups	tuning fork
funnels	boats
meat baster	objects that sink/float
egg beater	food coloring
rubber hose	liquid soap
squeeze bottles	watering can
corks	plastic containers
sponges	tubes
pans	metal/plastic measuring spoons
sieve	whisk
water pump	

THINGS TO KNOW:

1) Generally, heavy things sink, light ones float.
2) Hollow things float until they fill with water.
3) Water does not go up the baster unless you squeeze the bulb.
4) Blowing air into the pipe full of soapy water makes bubbles.
5) Sponges, cloth, and paper absorb water.
6) Water takes the shape of the container it is in.
7) Water has no color.
8) Using sets of measuring cups helps the child see relationships between volumes. Two red cups (½ cup each) fill 1 white cup (1 cup).

9) Water illustrates concepts of full and empty.
10) Water has weight and water weight helps things float.
11) Water goes into some things and not into others.

DOES WATER FEEL HEAVY?

YOU'LL NEED:

2 qt. pitcher   water
½ gallon milk carton   bucket

HERE'S HOW:

Pass a pitcher of water for the children to wet their fingers in. Do you think this clear water could be heavy?

Let the children fill an empty bucket. Keep lifting the bucket to test its weight. When it becomes hard to lift ask the children if it feels heavy. Empty some of the water out. Stop when it becomes light.

DO SOME THINGS WEIGH THE SAME DRY AND DAMP?

YOU'LL NEED:

matching set of small cups   sand
canisters   water
caps   sponges
tops   newspapers
½ pint milk cartons   scoops

HERE'S HOW:

Put an empty cup on the scale. How much does it weigh? Now let's add water to the cup. If the pointer moves down, what does it mean? Does the cup weigh more now since we added the water to it? How do you know?

Put dry sand in 2 matching cups. Weigh each to see that they are equal. Have the children put a little water in the sand cup on the scale. Where is the pointer now? Why do you think it moved? Check the weight of the sand cup again to verify the change in the damp sand weight. Let the children measure, weigh, and add water. Make a simple chart for the children to record weight of wet, damp or dry materials.

WILL SOME THINGS SINK, SOME FLOAT?

YOU'LL NEED:

dishpans of water   assorted objects
kitchen scale   large bucket of water
　　2 trays — label one tray "sink" and one tray "float"

HERE'S HOW:

Let the children play with the materials in a relaxed manner first. Then ask why the water holds some things up and not others. Will this ball stay on the top or will it sink to the bottom of the bucket? Encourage the children to weigh the different objects on a scale to confirm that objects can differ in weight, and act differently in water. Put out the sink/float trays. Ask the children to classify the objects.

Make a chart with accompanying work sheets to help the children record sinking and floating objects.

Will it sink? ⚓	Float? ⛵	
✺ leaf		
🪣 cork		
🥄 wooden spoon		
⚲ nail		
🎈 balloon		

HOW LONG WILL IT TAKE TO SINK?

YOU'LL NEED:

    stop watch   water container
    cloth   leaves
    various weights of paper (oaktag, paper towels, cardbaord, waxpaper)

HERE'S HOW:

    Drop items at different times and record the time it takes for them to sink.

Record Card

ITEM	TIME

Graph the answers:

TIME IN SECONDS

10   20   30   40   50

ITEMS

CARDBOARD
OAKTAG
WAXPAPER
CONSTRUCTION
PAPER
PAPER TOWEL

5

WHAT MAKES SOME THINGS FLOAT?

YOU'LL NEED:

dishpans of water

clear garden hose or tubing

plastic bottles

large bucket of water

2 corks to fit each hose

pill bottles with caps

HERE'S HOW:

Remove one cork from the hose. Submerge it in the water. Let it fill almost to the top. Replace cork. What do you think is in the hose now? Is air or water on the top? Which will be on the top if the hose is turned upside down? Let's try. Now drop 2 capped bottles into the water. What will happen if you take the cap off the bottle? Will it still float? What is in the bottle with the cap on it?

FOLLOW UP:

Read *The Story of Ping,* by Marjorie Flack.

FLOAT AN EGG!

YOU'LL NEED:

2 jars

3 Tablespoons of salt

1 shelled, hardboiled egg

HERE'S HOW:

1) Fill each jar halfway with water.
2) Dissolve salt in one jar.
3) Drop the egg in the jar of clear water. What happens?
4) Now drop the egg into the salt water. What has happened?

WHICH THINGS WILL ABSORB WATER?
(Step I)

YOU'LL NEED:

small funnel and baster

meat trays

sponge

wood

paper

tissues

dried clay

cotton

HERE'S HOW:

What happens when you put drops of water on the materials on your tray? Listen to childrens' ideas. Use the words "absorb" and "repel." Give a small cube of sponge to each child. Have him put it in a dry place. Squeeze water on to the sponge with the baster, and let the children observe what happens.

WHICH THINGS WILL ABSORB WATER?
(Step 2)

YOU'LL NEED:

6" square of cotton fabric
smooth feathers
leather scraps
water

plastic sheeting or rubberized fabric
waxed paper
spray bottle

HERE'S HOW:

Move from one child to another with a piece of dry fabric and the spray bottle. Drape the cloth over the child's arm. Ask: "What do you feel when I spray the cloth?" Repeat with the rubberized material. Give each child a feather to hold while you place one drop of water on the feather. Ask: "What do feathers do for birds?"

FOLLOW UP:

Read *Wet and Dry,* by Seymore Simon.

GROUP EXPERIENCE:

Put some dried beans into a plastic jar with lid. Let each child squeeze a dry bean and put it in a jar. How did it feel? Mark the level of the beans with a crayon. Pour in enough water to cover the beans. Cap the jar. Set aside a few beans for comparison. Next day, check the amount of space the beans take up in the jar. What do you notice has happened? Where did the water go?

WHICH THINGS DISSOLVE IN WATER?

YOU'LL NEED:

muffin tins
plastic ice cube trays
molds
pill containers

pitcher of water
spoons
small screw top bottle
salad oil

assorted materials: flour, sand, cornstarch, seeds, salt

HERE'S HOW:

See what happens when you put a little salt in one of your pans of water. Stir it. Can you see it? What do you think happened? Taste the water. Is it salty? We say the salt has *dissolved*. Try the other materials. What do you think will happen? Half fill the bottles with water. Add some oil. Secure and shake. Does the oil seem to dissolve? Let it stand for awhile. What has happened? Where is the oil?

FOLLOW UP:

Make a chart for recording the materials that dissolved and those that did not.

WHICH MOVES SLOWEST? FASTEST?

YOU'LL NEED:

4 baby food jars with lids   marker
4 marbles   rubber cement
construction paper   laminating paper
    clear liquid: water, light corn syrup, cooking oil, light corn syrup

HERE'S HOW:

Fill each jar with a different liquid. Place one marble in each jar. Glue the lids to the jars with the rubber cement. On the paper print: "Which moves fastest? Slowest?" Cover the sign with plastic laminating paper.

Allow the children to turn the bottles upside down. Which marble moved the fastest? Slowest? What do you think is inside each jar? What causes the marble to move at different speeds? Encourage the children to make their own bottles.

WHICH MOVES THE FASTEST?

PUT IT HERE

WHICH MOVES THE SLOWEST?

PUT IT HERE

   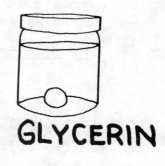

WATER   CORN SYRUP   COOKING OIL   GLYCERIN

MAKE WAVES!

YOU'LL NEED:

Clear bottle
rubbing alcohol

mineral oil
food coloring

HERE'S HOW:

1) Fill container halfway with mineral oil. Slowly pour in rubbing alcohol until the bottle is full.
2) Add a few drops of food colors.
3) Close the bottle and move it slowly back and forth.
4) Add small plastic toy boats or flowers to the children can observe that the items float in alcohol and sink in mineral oil.

DOES SOAP BREAK UP WATER'S SURFACE TENSION?

YOU'LL NEED:

pepper
talcum powder
pitcher of water
small jar

spoon
small pieces of soap
shallow foil pans
liquid detergent

HERE'S HOW:

Pour 1 inch of water in the foil pans. Fill the jar halfway with water. If we stir the pepper and water together in this jar, what do you think will happen? Will they mix if we gently sprinkle pepper on top of the water? What keeps the pepper on top of the water? (Surface tension.) Add some soap. Now what has happened? Experiment as you add liquid detergent. What happens when your clothes are washed? Why do you think we use soap?

EXPLORING ICE CUBES

YOU'LL NEED:

ice cubes   cups
small tins or ice cube trays   clock

HERE'S HOW:

1) Let's see who can make his ice cube melt the fastest. What can you do to make it melt? Time the melting process.
2) Give the children some crushed ice. Ask them to make it melt. Which ice melted more quickly, cubes or crushed?
3) Give the group three pans of water: hot, warm, cold. Ask them to choose the pan they think will melt their ice cubes the fastest. Test their predictions.
4) Freezing — Show three pans of water: hot, cold, warm. Which do you think will freeze first? Second? Third? Place the pans outdoors on a very cold day to test.

VARIATION:

Place some salt in one pan of water, pepper in another. Which do you think will freeze first? Test.

Fill a jar with water and mark the waterline. Place in the freezer. What happens to the waterline? Melt the ice. What has happened to the waterline now? Why?

Float an ice cube on water and observe how much of the ice shows above the surface.

OBSERVING WATER

YOU'LL NEED:

baby food jars   plastic flowers
scissors   2 " square of aluminum foil
tape   clay

HERE'S HOW:

1) Place clay in the bottom of a jar lid. Place the plastic flower in the clay.
2) Cut tiny squares of foil.
3) Fill the jar with water. Put foil squares in the jar.
4) Close the jar tightly.
5) Shake jar and observe what happens.

VARIATION:

Omit foil squares and use soap flakes!

COLORED SOLUTIONS

YOU'LL NEED:

plastic tubes or jars
eyedroppers
food coloring

water
salt
pails or containers of water

HERE'S HOW:

Give the children eyedroppers and food coloring to add to the water What will happen to the water? Stir the water. Now what has happened? How could we make the color darker? If you add another color what will happen? Try and see.

Try dropping color into *hot* water. Is there a difference?

Mix salt, water and food coloring. Have the children drop the mixture into plain water. Now what do you see?

CLAY BOATS

INTRODUCTION:

In this activity the children investigate the possibilities of making a small ball of clay float in a container of water. They will make clay shapes and fill them with small objects to find how much "cargo" the boat will hold. They will eventually change the shape of the boats and observe which boats float most successfully.

YOU'LL NEED:

clay
marbles
washers

water table or tub
papercups
plastic cups

HERE'S HOW:

Roll your clay into a ball. What do you think will happen when you drop it into the water? Put the clay into the water. What happened? What do you think you could do to make it float?

Allow the children to experiment. Some may wish to try a larger container of water. When they discover a shape that floats, try loading a boat. Find out which boats hold the most.

FOLLOW UP:

Float a plastic cup next to the clay boat. Add weighted objects to the boat, counting to see how many it will hold. Ask the children to predict how many things they think the cup will hold. Repeat to see if the capacity of the cup is fairly constant. Which held the most, the boat or the cup?

HOT AND COLD

INTRODUCTION:

Read *Hot and Cold,* by Catherine Chase, Dandelion Books, New York, 1979.

HERE'S HOW:

Fill three bowls about halfway with hot, cold, and warm water.

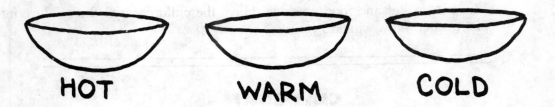

HOT   WARM   COLD

Put your left hand in the bowl of hot water, right hand in the bowl of cold. Wait one minute. Put both hands in this middle bowl. How does it feel? How does your right hand feel? Your left? Why? (Reason: When something feels hot or cool or cold, you are feeling the flow of heat. Heat flows from something warmer to something cooler.)

Hold an ice cube in your hand. What happens? How does it feel? Your hand is warmer than the ice cube. Heat flows from your hand to the ice. You do not feel cold from the ice cube. You lose heat to the ice cube.

PREDICTING WATER LEVELS

YOU'LL NEED:

jars   rubber bands
markers   stones

HERE'S HOW:

Mark the water level in a jar of water. Drop in a stone. Place a rubber band around the new level.

Ask the children to predict how high the level will rise with different sized stones. Place a rubber band on the jar to note each prediction.

BATH TUB SCIENCE – HOME ACTIVITIES

INTRODUCTION:

These are activities for parents and children to do at home while the child is in the bathtub.

YOU'LL NEED:

sponges   whisk
meat baster   eggbeater
boats   soap bubbles
squeeze bottles   plastic pitcher
tubes   rubber animals

HERE'S HOW:

Keep the toys in a net stocking or onion bag. This way they can be hung up after use and they will be dry and ready for water play when bath time rolls around again. Take extra care of metal equipment.

ACTIVITIES:

1) Ask the child to find out which materials sink/float.
2) Use pitchers for pouring and measuring. Talk about the meaning of *full/empty*.
3) How can we make bubbles? What are bubbles? What pictures can you see in soap bubbles?
4) Fill tubes and bottles with water. Talk about which has *more*, which has *less*.
5) Float an ice cube in the water. What happens to your water? Talk about *cold, warm, hot*.
6) Put equal amounts of water in 2 cups. Now pour one into a tall thin tube. Do they still have the same amount of water, or does one have more?

7) Can you fill a container with soap bubbles? Now fill another container with water. Which one is heavier? Talk about *heavy* and *light*.

8) Float a plastic container in the water. Begin adding rubber animals. How many animals can we put into our "boat" before it sinks or turns over?

9) Can you make waves in the tub? A whirlpool? Put a duck in the water. Make circular motions around it. What happens to the duck?

10) Put drops of water on your skin. Watch them dry. Talk about *wet/dry*. What makes you get dry?

11) How do you feel when you get out of a hot tub? Why do you actually feel cold?

EXTRA! EXTRA!

1) Teach "Row, Row, Row Your Boat, " and "Michael, Row Your Boat Ashore." Use the large wooden Community Playthings boat for dramatization. What holds our boat up?

2) Where do we get our rain? Make rain by boiling a kettle of water and covering it with a cold lid. Teach the song, "The Eency Weency Spider." How did the rain dry up?

3) Demonstrate how water can turn solids into liquids. Dissolve sugar, salt, dry mild crystals into water.

4) Why do we need water? Find out what happens when a plant is not watered.

5) Let the children taste ocean water, spring water, snow, and mineral water.

6) MATH ACTIVITY: Encourage the children to count aloud the number of stirs each child takes when dissolving drink mixes or jello in water.

7) Provide a set of measuring cups: 4 oz., 8 oz., 16 oz., or 3 sizes of paper milk cartons, for use by the children playing with water. Ask how many small containers it takes to fill a large container.

8) ART ACTIVITY: Allow the children to mix paint to find new colors. Try blending colors with a wire wisk.

Ice Cube Painting — Use finger paint and glossy paper but do not wet the paper. Give the children ice cubes to use to spread their paint around the paper.

Rain, Rain Collage — Make a picture on construction paper with glue. Sprinkle confetti or paper punches over the sticky area. Add magazine pictures of flowers and plants.

9) DRAMATIC PLAY: Wash dolls and doll clothes. Hang them up to dry. Where do you think they will dry the fastest?

In warm weather, let the children get their feet wet and make footprints on concrete. Whose feet are the smallest, the biggest?

Making Bubbles — On a windy day give the children commercial bubble solution and let them blow bubbles outside.

Give the children milk cartons half full of water and liquid detergent. What color would you like your bubbles to be? Add a few drops of the appropriate food coloring. Give each child a straw. Practice blowing *out* before putting the straw into the soapy water. Colored bubbles!

Try using small plastic funnels to blow giant bubbles. Put the funnel upside down in a bowl of detergent solution. Gently blow a few bubbles into the bowl to allow a film of solution to coat the inside of the funnel.

Winter

Icy, white flakes falling
Shrill, red cardinals calling.
Tiny footprints scurrying,
Bundled shoppers hurrying.
Fierce, gray wind a blowing,
Happy children knowing,
It's winter!

Snow

One flake drifting in the air,
Lights on lashes, nose and hair,
Calls to the children, "Come and play with me,
My fellow flakes are falling, we don't stay long, you see."
We're only here a short time, come and join the fun.
Romp and play, enjoy the day, and hide from Mr. Sun! "

Rain

Up with your umbrella!
Here comes the rain!
Beating on the sidewalks, washing window panes.
Catch a tine droplet, there's life inside each one,
Nature in abundance,
Now drying in the sun.

Poetry by Terry Lynne Graham.

Children's Literature

Bright, Robert. *Georgie and the Noisy Ghost.* N.Y.: Scholastic Book Services, 1972.
Holt, Adelaide. *The Rain Puddle.* N.Y.: 1965 (Evaporation)
Keats, Ezra Jack. *The Snowy Day.* N.Y.: Viking Press, 1962. (Melting)
Koch, Dorothy. *Let it Rain.* N.Y.: Holiday House, 1969. (Surface tension, absorption, water repellency)
Milgram, Harry. *ABC Science Experiments.* N.Y.: Macmillan Co., 1970.
Rey, H.A. *Curious George Rides a Bike.* N.Y.: Scholastic Book Service, 1973. (Floating paper boats)

Rosenfeld, Sam. *A Drop of Water.* N.Y.: Harvey House, 1970. (Water cycle)

Schulevits, Uri. *Rain, Rain, Rivers.* N.Y.: Farrar, Straus, and Giroux, 1969. (What do children, birds, and plants get from rain)

Tresselt, Alvin. *Hide and Seek Fog.* N.Y.: Lothrop, Lee and Shepard Co., 1965.

Poetry

"Dragon Smoke," by Lillian More

"Weather," by Eve Merriam

"Galoshes," by Rhoda Bacmeister

Now We Are Six, by A.A. Milne, "Waiting at the Window"

Poems to Grow On, by Jean Thompson. Includes "The Snowflake" by Walter de la Mare.

Resources

Danoff, Judith. *Open for Children.* N.Y.: McGraw Hill, 1977.

Debelak, Marianne, Judith Herr, Martha Jacobson. *Creating Innovative Classroom Materials for Young Children.* N.Y.: Harcourt, Brace, Jovanovich, Inc., 1981.

Harlan, Jean Durgin. *Science Experiences for the Early Years.* Columbus, O.: Charles C. Merrill Co., 1976.

Menlove, Coleen. *Ready, Set, Go!* Englewood Cliffs, N.J.: Prentice Hall, 1978.

Chapter Two

A · I · R

What is air and how do we know it's there? You blow on hot soup to cool it off and in winter you blow on your hands to make them warmer. Air is all around us and yet we cannot see it! One thing we can say, air is a puzzlement!

Help children put that puzzle together by exploring the properties of air, and their discoveries will lead to an understanding. The activities here touch on air pressure and changes, condensation, movement and weight. Task cards are included to incorporate into a learning center, and a special section will aid in establishing a learning center on "Air Pollution."

What Is It?

> You cannot see it.
> You cannot taste it.
> You cannot smell it.
> And —
> you cannot live without it.
> Elephants and tigers,
> Fish and birds,
> Butterflies and snails,
> Even snakes and worms —
> no animal can live without it.
> No plant can live without it.
> What is it? *

* *Air All Around* by Tillie S. Pine and Joseph Levine, McGraw Hill Book Co., 1960.

19

Discovering & Exploring Air

SETTING UP AN "AIR DEPARTMENT"

EQUIPMENT:

balloons
glasses
string
thermometer
pans
pins

straws
funnel
bottles
newspaper
plastic ball

THINGS TO KNOW:

1) You can feel air
2) Air has space, weight, pressure
3) Air is used for transportation
4) Air can be heard, you can stretch air
5) Air moves — it rises and falls

CAN YOU FEEL AIR?

YOU'LL NEED:

balloons
paper for fans

electric fan

HERE'S HOW:

Blow up balloons. Let air escape against face. Have electric fan blow air against body. Make paper fans and fan each other. Ask: "Can you feel air?"

AIR HAS SPACE

YOU'LL NEED:

glass
bowl of water

paper napkin

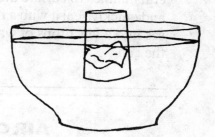

HERE'S HOW:

Place napkin in glass then put glass into the water. Why didn't the napkin get wet? Does air take up space?

AIR HAS WEIGHT

YOU'LL NEED:

2 balloons
string

small dowel

HERE'S HOW:

Blow up the balloons and attach to dowel with string. Let air out of one balloon. Does air have weight?

AIR HAS PRESSURE

YOU'LL NEED:

suction dart game
glass and piece of cardboard
gallon can

plumber's force cup
glass and 2 drinking straws

HERE'S HOW:

Play dart game. Why do darts stick?

Press plumber's force cup to wall. Ask same question.

Fill glass with water. Cover with cardboard and turn upside down. Why doesn't the water come out?

Try drinking water with one straw inside glass and one on outside. Why doesn't it work?

Boil a small amount of water in the gallon can. Allow the water to boil for several minutes to be sure the steam drives the air out of the can. Remove the can and quickly seal it with a rubber stopper. As steam inside can cools, it condenses into a few drops of water and creates a vacuum. The air pressure crushes the can.

AIR CAN BE HEARD

YOU'LL NEED:

horn   can of food
can opener

HERE'S HOW:

Blow horn. What do you hear?
Listen for air sounds when can opener punctures can.

CHANGES IN AIR

YOU'LL NEED:

thermometer   temperature chart
hot plate   pan of water

HERE'S HOW:

Record indoor and outdoor temperature on chart. Heat pan of water. Feel the hot air. Where does it go?
Make a bulletin board of pictures showing hot climates and cold climates, etc.

TEMPERATURE CHART		
DATE	INSIDE	OUTSIDE

HOW DOES AIR DRY?

YOU'LL NEED:

hairdryer   doll with hair
electric fan   doll's clothes
small clothes line

HERE'S HOW:

Wet doll's hair then blow with hair dryer.
Wash" doll's clothes, hang on clothes line, and place in front of electric fan.
Ask: "Can air dry things?"

WIND IS MOVING AIR;
IT CHANGES IN FORCE AND DIRECTION

YOU'LL NEED:

electric fan   streamers
toy sailboat in pan of water
for pinwheel
6" squares of paper   scissors
pins   pencils with erasers at end

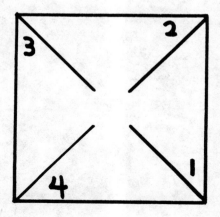

HERE'S HOW:

Blow against sails of boat.

Attach streamers to electric fan. Turn on fan.

Make pinwheels by folding down corners 1, 2, 3, and 4 to center of page. Put a pin through corners and stick it into the eraser at the end of the pencil.

Task Cards

task card #1

YOU'LL NEED:

    straws   glass of water
    soil   cup
    plastic bag

HERE'S HOW:

1) Take a straw. Blow into a glass of water. Describe what you see and why.

2) Put some soil in a cup. Make sure the soil is dry. Pour a little water over the soil. What happened? What did you see? Record your answer.

3) Take a small plastic bag and wave it in the air a few times. Close the bag quickly. Describe what happened to the bag and why.

task card #2

YOU'LL NEED:

    straw   balloon
    cup of water   glue
    piece of rubber   toothpick
    funnel   scale

HERE'S HOW:

1) Put a short straw in a cup of water. Hold it there. Take a longer straw and, holding it perpendicular to and above the short straw, blow directly over the top of the short straw. Watch what happens. See if you can explain why to someone.

2) Cover the mouth of a funnel with a piece of rubber. Suck some air from the narrow end of the funnel and notice what happens to the rubber. Turn the funnel upside down and suck in again. Then turn the funnel sideways and suck in. Record your discovery. Discuss it with someone.

3) Hold your nose and try to breath out (through your nose). Do not try this too hard for it will hurt your ears. Describe to your teacher how it feels.

task card #3

YOU'LL NEED:

balloon   string
refrigerator

HERE'S HOW:

1) Blow up a balloon. Measure the distance around (circumference) with a string.
Record your measurement. Place the balloon in the cold part of the refrigerator.
Let it stand for a while. Take it out and measure the balloon again. Observe the
balloon and compare your findings.

task card #4

YOU'LL NEED:

bottle   pail of water
dime   hot water

HERE'S HOW:

1) Use a bottle from the table that has a small opening. Set the bottle in a pail of very
cold water. Take the bottle out, making sure that the rim is moist. Place a dime on
the rim. Make sure the dime covers the entire rim. Hold your hands around the
lower part of the bottle. Take your hands away. Put them back on the bottle again.
Record what happened. See if you can state why.
2) Stretch a balloon over the neck of a bottle of hot water. Record what happens to
the balloon as you watch it.

task card # 5

YOU'LL NEED:

shiny can   ice cubes
water

HERE'S HOW:

1) Put some water in a shiny tin can and add some ice cubes. Let it stand for a while. Look at the can. What do you see happening? Why? Report your observations to your teacher. Relate this experiment to something that happens with the weather.

task card # 6

YOU'LL NEED:

talcum powder   cloth
lamp

HERE'S HOW:

1) Sprinkle talcum powder on a cloth. Shake some of the powder off near a lamp. Watch what happens to the powder. Turn the lamp on and give it a few minutes to get hot. Shake some more powder off the cloth. Watch what happens this time. Record your findings and state why.

task card #7

YOU'LL NEED:

newspaper
glass
plastic ball
water

plastic jar
gallon jar
balloon

HERE'S HOW:

1) Stuff some crumpled newspaper into an empty glass. Make sure the paper is stuffed in tightly so it will not fall out when you turn the glass upside down. Fill a plastic pail with water. Hold the mouth of the glass down and put the glass deep into the pail. Hold it there for a minute or two. Pull the glass out of the water and remove the paper. Observe the paper. Write what happened and explain why.

2) Take a plastic bag and tie the opening tightly over the mouth of a gallon jar, with the bag inside the jar. Hold the jar and pull the bag out. Watch what happened. Explain this to one of your classmates.

3) Blow up a balloon. Describe why the balloon stays inflated. Deflate the balloon. Describe the balloon now. Discuss this with your teacher.

task card #8

YOU'LL NEED:

plastic bag
dish
deep bowl of water

book
glass
sand

HERE'S HOW:

1) Place a plastic bag on a desk with the open end over the edge. Place a book on the bag. Blow into the bag. See what happens to the book. Add more books and blow up the bag. Record what happens.

2) Hold a glass with the mouth down. Push it into a deep bowl of water. Describe what you see. Explain your findings in a few sentences.

3) Put a little sand in a plastic bag, then, fill it with air. Pop the bag. Describe what happened to the sand. Make a record of what happened.

task card #9

YOU'LL NEED:

  newsprint

HERE'S HOW:

1) Use two pieces of newsprint for the experiment. Crumple one into a ball. Lift your arms high and drop both pieces of paper at the same time. Observe what happens. Explain why to your classmates.

task card #10

YOU'LL NEED:

  string   yardstick
  balloon   paper

HERE'S HOW:

1) Tie a string around the middle of a yardstick. Attach the yardstick horizontally to the top of the back of a chair. Blow up a large balloon. Tie it tightly and hang it on the one inch mark of the yardstick. Roll up some papers and tie them together with a string. Tie the string on the 35 inch marker of the yardstick. Add or remove paper until the stick balances. Then let the air out of the balloon. Describe what happened. Can you explain why? Record your findings.

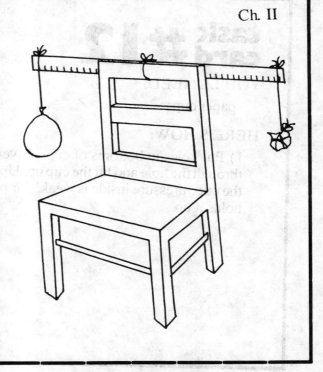

task card # 11

YOU'LL NEED:

empty soda bottle
clay

straws
water

HERE'S HOW:

1) Fill soda bottle with water and *smooth clay around one end of the straw.* Challenge the children to suck from the straw. Take away some of the clay. Watch the water come up! Air presses down on the water and pulls up the straw.

task card # 12

YOU'LL NEED:

paper cups

small pieces of paper

HERE'S HOW:

1) Put holes in bottoms of cups. Invert cups over paper and have children suck through the hole and lift the cup up. Up comes the paper! When they suck air from the cup, pressure inside is weak. Air outside the cup presses under the paper and holds it up.

task card #13

YOU'LL NEED:

   empty soda bottles   straws
   tape   water

HERE'S HOW:

1) Tape several straws together end to end. Fill bottles and let children insert tall straws to see how high the water will come up.

task card #14

YOU'LL NEED:

   jar   cover
   ice cubes

HERE'S HOW:

1) Fill jar with ice and put on cover. Drops of water form from air outside. The water in air forms drops when air around jar cools off.

task card #15

YOU'LL NEED:

paper bags   books

HERE'S HOW:

1) Make neck in a bag. Stand the book on the bag. Hold neck and blow air into bag, which pushes on book: down goes the book!

task card #16

YOU'LL NEED:

piece of paper   glass of water

HERE'S HOW:

1) Press paper tightly to top of glass so that no air can get in. Turn glass over. The paper will not fall off or the water run out. Air pushes on the paper and holds the water in.

task card # 17

YOU'LL NEED:
    glasses   balloon

HERE'S HOW:
   1) Put a balloon in a glass. Child blows up the balloon. The air in the balloon pushes hard on the sides of the glass, and child can pick up the glass with a balloon.

task card # 18

YOU'LL NEED:
    straws   water

HERE'S HOW:
   1) Put a finger over one end of a straw. Fill the straw with water. Put a finger on top of the straw and remove the finger from the bottom. Air keeps the water from running out of the straw. Remove finger, and air gets in, water runs out. Air pushes in all directions.

task card # 19

YOU'LL NEED:

spool   Scotch tape
straw   heavy paper
hat pin

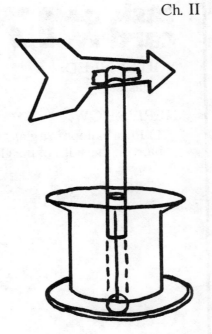

HERE'S HOW:

1) Stick the straw vertically into the spool. Insert the hat pin through the paper at the bottom of the spool and up through the straw. Scotch tape an arrow made of heavy paper to the top of the straw, perpendicular to the straw. The vane will point to the direction from which the wind is coming.

task card # 20

YOU'LL NEED:

empty milk cartons   small pieces of paper

HERE'S HOW:

Hold open end of milk carton near face and squeeze and feel the air. Put the papers on a table. To show that air takes up space and air moves, squeeze carton and watch the papers scatter.

Learning Center in Air Pollution

OBJECTIVE:

To provide through observation and experimentation experiences in what air pollution is and what it does, and to determine what the alternatives are.

INTRODUCTION:

What is air pollution? (Dirty air.)

Who or what causes air pollution? (Man-made sources: factories, cars, trucks, buses, airplanes, burning of fuel for heat, power, construction, manufacturing, garbage disposal, burning leaves. Natural Sources: dust carried by the wind, salt from ocean spray, smoke from forest fires and volcanoes, swamp and ocean gases.)

PARTICLES IN THE AIR
(smoke, soot, dust)

YOU'LL NEED:

14 white index cards	vaseline
tape	magnifying lens

HERE'S HOW:

Spread thin layer of vaseline on cards. Tape 7 cards outside and 7 cards inside by a window. Each day, remove one card from each set and make observations with lens. Start a chart and record all observations.

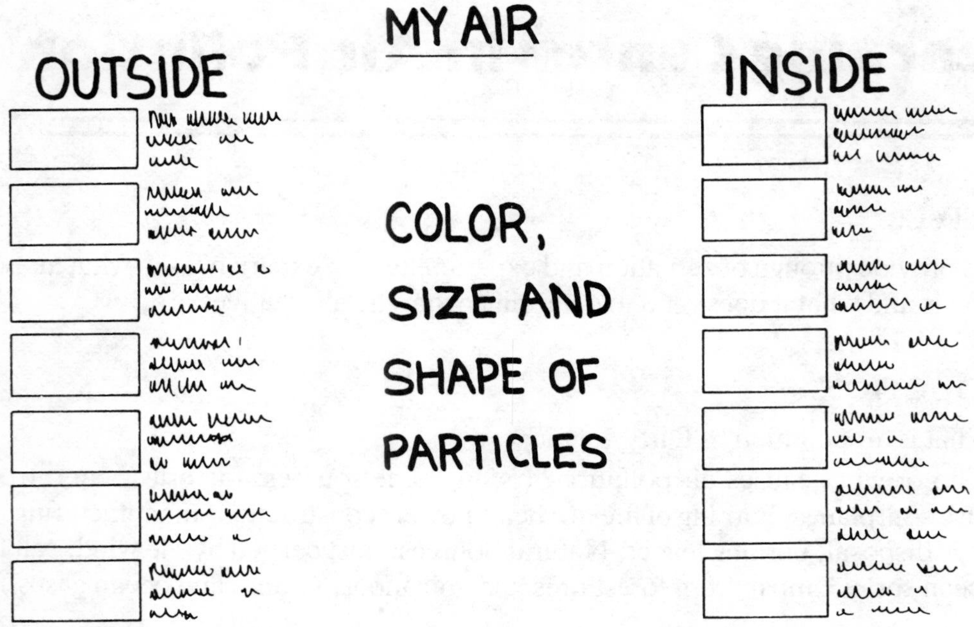
MY AIR
OUTSIDE
INSIDE
COLOR,
SIZE AND
SHAPE OF
PARTICLES

MY AIR

YOU'LL NEED:

rug or dust cloth

HERE'S HOW:

Darken room, shine flashlight, and shake out rug into light beam. Observe and discuss what you see.

CAUSES OF AIR POLLUTION (1)
(Cars and Gases — invisible pollution)

YOU'LL NEED:

white index cards   vaseline
magnifying lens   exhausts from several cars (all ages and types)

HERE'S HOW:

Spread cards with thin layer of vaseline. Place card 1 foot from exhaust pipe of car being tested. Note year, make and type of car and date of last tune-up.

Make observations with lens and prepare a chart with recorded observations similar to the one used in Particles in the Air, Activity # 1.

CAUSES OF AIR POLLUTION (2)
(Burning of Fuel)

YOU'LL NEED:

4 candles   2 medium-sized glass jars

HERE'S HOW:

Light candles. Hold a jar upside down over one candle and the other jar over three candles for about 30 seconds. Extinguish flames. Compare soot deposited in each jar. Which caused more soot? Why? What does this tell us about engine power? Frequent use of cars for short trips?

CAUSES OF AIR POLLUTION (3)
(Cars and Trucks)

YOU'LL NEED:

vaseline
durable tape

several 3" x 5" cards
a nearby intersection

HERE'S HOW:

Take a trip to a busy traffic intersection to note visible signs of pollution. Vaseline-covered cards can be taped nearby and retrieved in a few days for observation. Do the same at a not so busy intersection and compare.

SMOKE (1)

YOU'LL NEED:

2 two inch squares of Kleenex tissue (3 layers thick)
cigarettes (1 filtered and 1 unfiltered)

matches

HERE'S HOW:

Place tissue paper squares over the end to be smoked and have an adult smoke a few puffs from each cigarette. Observe what happens to the tissue paper. Open the cigarette's filter and examine it.

SMOKE (2)

YOU'LL NEED:

cigarette
flashlight

matches

HERE'S HOW:

Darken room while adult smokes a cigarette. Observe smoke in flashlight beam. Who is polluting the air? Who is breathing this air?

SMOKE (3)

YOU'LL NEED:

jar   matches
2 dry leaves

HERE'S HOW:

Set leaves on fire and put in jar. Cover with lid. When fire is out, open jar.
Observe amount of smoke and soot deposited in jar and inside lid. All from
only 2 burning leaves!

SMOKE (4)

YOU'LL NEED:

a nearby factory   sharp eyes
vaseline   several 3'' x 5'' cards

HERE'S HOW:

Take a trip to a nearby factory and observe possible signs of pollution. Place
vaseline-covered cards nearby for study.

SMOG AND TEMPERATURE INVERSION

YOU'LL NEED:

½ gallon jar with narrow mouth   match
water

HERE'S HOW:

Cover bottom of jar with water and moisten all sides of jar. Light a match and
throw it into the jar. Place your mouth over the top of jar and blow hard into it.
Hold your breath for a few seconds and you've created a temperature inver-
sion. (Smog and fog on cool surface, air being held down by warm air above.)

FOLLOW UP:

Have children draw pictures of pollution. Put them on display.
Have children classify pictures they cut from magazines into following categories:

Invisible Pollution and Visible Pollution

Pollution and Alternatives (picture of bicycle rider as alternative to automobile; nonsmoker as alternative to smoker; etc.)

Make suggestions for a list of new words children have learned during these activities.

Resources

Croft, Doreen J. and Robert D. Hess. *An Activities Book for Teachers of Young Children.* Hopewell, N.J.: Houghton Mifflin Co., 1975.

General Motors Corp. *Professor Clean Asks... What is Air Pollution?* Detroit, Mich.: 1973.

McDonald's Corp. *Ecology Action Pack.* Kettering, O.: 1975.

Menlove, Coleen Kent. *Ready, Set, Go.* Englewood Cliffs, N.J.: Spectrum Books, 1978.

Perera, Thomas B. and Wallace Orlowsky. *Who Will Clean the Air?* N.Y.: Cowen, McCann and Geoghegan, Inc., 1971.

Simon, Seymour. *Science Projects in Pollution.* N.Y.: Holiday Publishing.

Film:

The Lorax. Dr. Seuss, 25 minutes

Free Materials:

Woodsy Owl Environmental Education Teacher's Kit. Woodsy Owl Forest Service. U.S.D.A. – P.O. Box 1963. Washington, D.C. 20013. 1977. Single copy free to teachers. Materials included are an introduction to environmental education, a poster, bookmark, wallet card, song sheet, and coloring sheet. Elem.

Air Pollution. American Lung Association – 1740 Broadway. New York, N.Y. 10019. Several materials which present the effects of air pollution of the environment and on one's health are available free. Send for catalog. Sample titles are: Air Pollution Primer. No. 4010. 1974. 104 pp.

GPO Materials. U.S. Government Printing Office. Washington, D.C. 20402. Lists of many low-cost government publications which may be used in the classroom.

Once There Lived a Wicked Dragon. 1975. 32 p. Free. Story book to teacher children about ecology; includes pictures to color.

Environmental Projects. Keep America Beautiful. 99 Park Ave. New York, N.Y. 10016. Free. A variety of materials for community and school projects to protect and improve the environment.

Chapter Three

P · L · A · N · T · S
& Growth

Baby Seeds

In a milkweed cradle,
Snug and warm
Baby seeds are hiding,
Safe from harm
Open wide the cradle,
Hold it high!
Come Mr. Wind,
Help them fly!

Anonymous

The inborn curiosity of young children makes plant and growth discovery a natural topic for the classroom. Begin by keeping flowers, cacti, and other plants that can be cared for easily in the classroom throughout the year. Give the children the responsibility for the plant's care. Discuss the growth and changes on a daily basis, and record your observations. Experience with plants and seeds gives children a basic understanding of life processes. These young gardeners will also experience a sense of pride and accomplishment when they've made something grow!

Discovering & Exploring Plants & Growth

SETTING UP A "GARDEN CENTER"

EQUIPMENT:

watering can
eyedroppers
spray bottle
milk cartons
potting soil

cups
paper towels
magnifying glass
trowel
variety of seeds

THINGS TO KNOW:

1) There are many types of seeds.
2) Each particular seed grows into a specific kind of plant.
3) Plants have roots, stems, and leaves.
4) Some plants grow from roots and stems.
5) Plants need light, water, air and soil to grow.

MILK CARTON GARDEN

YOU'LL NEED:

milk carton
seeds of any kind

Saran wrap
tape

potting soil

HERE'S HOW:

Cut off the top of the milk carton and cut windows in each side. Line the inside with Saran Wrap and tape in in place. Plant seeds next to the windows. Can you see the roots?

THE SOCK GARDEN

Where do you think we could find seeds?

YOU'LL NEED:

large plastic milk containers, cut in half
one large sock for each child
potting soil

Insert Sock Illustration

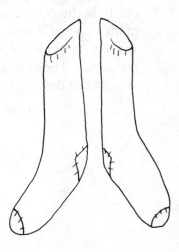

HERE'S HOW:

Have each child put on a sock over his shoe. Now you're ready for a Fall walk. Try to explore a wooded area. When you return, plant the socks in the milk cartons filled with soil. Can you draw a picture of what you think will grow? If you have collected any seeds, some plants should grow.

EXPERIENCE STORY:

Noah said, "First we put the socks over our shoes." Andrew said, "We went outside and stamped our socks in the mud." We wanted to pick flowers, seeds, and leaves, " said Jonathon. "We put dirt and our socks in a plastic container," said Elliot. Amanda thinks a flower will grow. Drew thinks a sock will grow! What do you think?

JACK'S BEANSTALK

INTRODUCTION:

Read the story of *Jack and the Beanstalk*. Would you like a beanstalk of your own?

YOU'LL NEED:

milk cartons
lima beans
yarn
spray water bottle

I WATERED MY BEANSTALK					
NAME	MON.	TUES.	WED.	THUR.	FRI.
MIKE	X				
TERRY		X	X		
JACK					

HERE'S HOW:

Fill the bottom of the carton with yarn. Dampen the yarn and place the bean on top. Keep the bean watered and near sunlight. Place this chart near your plants. When plants show significant growth, transplant them into soil.

HAPPY/SAD HARRY

YOU'LL NEED:

grass seed   paper cups
construction paper circles   crayons
potting soil   stapler
spray water bottle

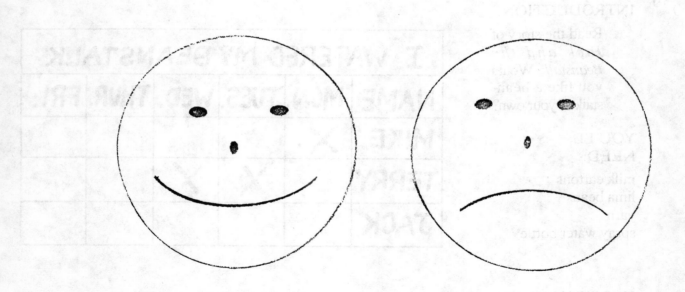

44

HERE'S HOW:

Place some grass seed in a bowl for the children to look at. Have you ever seen these seeds before? How do they look, feel, and smell? Ask the children to use the circles to draw one happy face and one sad face.

Staple the faces to the paper cups. Fill the cup with potting soil, almost to the top. Sprinkle on the grass seed. Place the cups in a sunny window and keep the soil moist. Watch Harry's green hair grow! Use the same type of chart as in the preceding activity to record watering.

GRASS GRAPH

INTRODUCTION:

Before the children take their cups of grass home, graph the growth of the grass.

HERE'S HOW:

Divide the class into three groups of about eight children each. Put the cups in a row and decide whose grass is the shortest, second shortest, up to the longest. Cut strips of paper to represent the relative height of each child's cup of grass.

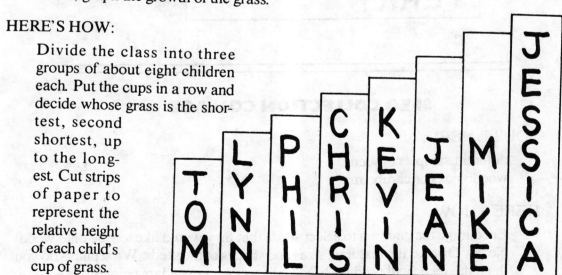

45

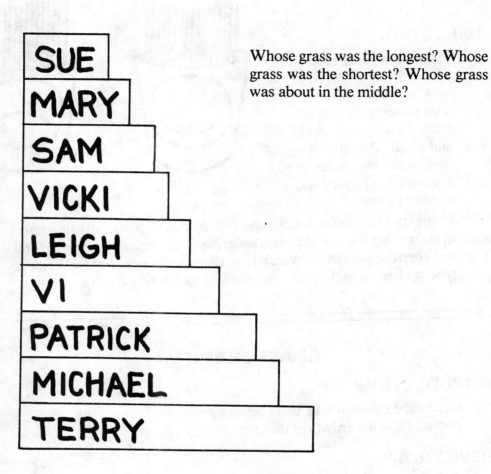

Whose grass was the longest? Whose grass was the shortest? Whose grass was about in the middle?

SEED COLLECTION COLLAGE

YOU'LL NEED:

different samples of seeds   glue
woodblocks or cardboard

HERE'S HOW:

Encourage the children to select seeds that they would like to glue onto woodblocks. Discuss the textures, sizes and shapes of the seeds. What plants do you think the seeds will produce? Do large seeds produce large plants?

OBSERVING GROWTH

YOU'LL NEED:

3 beans   magic marker
3 clear plastic cups
potting soil

HERE'S HOW:

Plant a bean seed in each cup, near the side. Label the cups: #1, #2, and #3. Put cups #1 and #3 in a sunny place. Water cups #1 and #3. Which seeds will grow best? Chart your predictions.
Fill in this chart:

PLANTS NEED

1.
2.
3.
4.

OUR PREDICTIONS

1 —

2 —

3 —

MOLD GARDEN

YOU'LL NEED:

a large aquarium
cheese

orange
bread

47

HERE'S HOW:

Place the foods in the aquarium. Set the aquarium in a warm place. Observe it for a few days. What has happened? Did we use seeds?

ECOLOGY GARDEN

YOU'LL NEED:

a large aquarium
spray water bottle

soil
seeds

HERE'S HOW:

Fill the aquarium with soil. Encourage the children to place apples, orange, and grape seeds from their snacks or lunches into the tank. Keep it moist and plants will grow!

ROOTING PLANTS

INTRODUCTION:

Did you know that carrots, sweet potatoes, and onions are the roots of plants? Try this activity!

YOU'LL NEED:

a sweet potato
toothpicks

glass
water

DAY 1	DAY 2	DAY 3	DAY 4	DAY 5

HERE'S HOW:

Stick the toothpicks into the potato. These will form a support to hold the potato near the top of the glass, pointed end down. Fill the glass with water and place it in a sunny corner. Record what happens.

ROOTING PLANTS (II)

YOU'LL NEED:

carrots	turnips
pineapple	pie tin of water

HERE'S HOW:

Cut off all but an inch of the green tops of your fruit or vegetable. Place the root in the pie tin. Add water. Place the root down. Do you think the root will grow?

PLANT TALK

YOU'LL NEED:

spider plant	zebra plant
a pussy willow	

HERE'S HOW:

Divide the class into three groups for discussion. Have each group observe one plant. Tell the children: "Think of as many attributes as you can to describe the plant (texture, size, shape, smell). What name would you give the plant?" Tell the children the true names of each plant. Ask, "Why do the names fit?"

HOW DO SEEDS TRAVEL?

INTRODUCTION:

Read the poem, "Baby Seeds" at the beginning of this chapter.

YOU'LL NEED:

milkweed pods	dandelion (going to seed)

HERE'S HOW:

Divide the class into small groups and let them open the milkweed pods. Find the seeds inside. Look closely at the dandelion. Do you see the seeds? If we take them outside, what do you think would happen? Take them out on a windy day to find out. What are other ways that seeds might travel?

FOLLOW UP:

Listen to "How Do Seeds of Plants Travel?" on the record *Now We Know*, (*Songs To Learn By*) by Tom Glaser, Columbia Records.

THINGS TO KNOW ABOUT TREES AND LEAVES:

1) Trees have specific names.
2) Trees have different leaves and different bark, and they come in various sizes and shapes.
3) Many trees lose their leaves in the winter.
4) In the spring, some trees get leaves first and some trees may get blossoms.
5) The rings in the grain of the wood tell us the age of the tree.

PARTS OF THE TREE

YOU'LL NEED:

white pelon
green magic marker

black pelon

HERE'S HOW:

Cut these shapes from the white pelon. Color the leaves green.

Cut this shape from the black pelon:

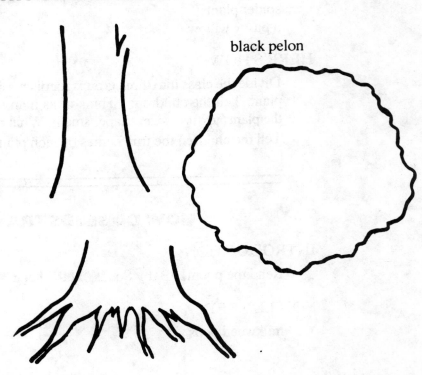

50

Place the pieces on the flannel board. Let the children put them together to create a tree. What are the parts called? What does each part do? Where are the *branches, leaves, bark?*

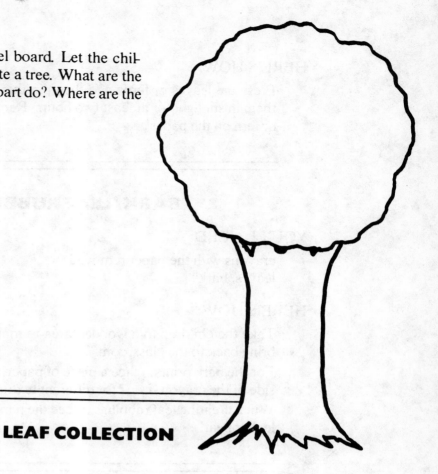

LEAF COLLECTION

YOU'LL NEED:

cardboard
clear contact paper

rubber cement

HERE'S HOW:

Have the children collect as many different leaves as they can. Mount them on the cardboard and cover them with clear contact paper.

In small groups discuss the names of all the leaves. Then try:
- Placing all the same leaves together.
- Placing the leaves in order according to size.
- Placing big/small leaves together.
- Counting all the leaves in the collection.

LEAF AND FERN PRINTS

YOU'LL NEED:

leaves
construction paper

ferns
pins

51

HERE'S HOW:

Press the leaves or ferns and then pin them to the construction paper. Place them in sunlight for at least two hours. Remove and observe a print of the leaf or fern on the paper!

BARK/LEAF RUBBINGS

YOU'LL NEED:

crayons with the paper removed   paper
leaves/bark

HERE'S HOW:

Take the children to a wooded area to make bark prints and gather leaves to bring back to the classroom.

For the bark prints, place a piece of paper up against the tree and rub with the side of the crayon. Look for different textures of bark.

When creating leaf rubbings, place the paper over the leaf and rub. Watch the leaf appear!

BUILDING A TERRARIUM

YOU'LL NEED:

a large aquarium   small stones or gravel
potting soil   spray water bottle
plants

HERE'S HOW:

Place the aquarium near the sunlight, but not in direct light. Put gravel along the bottom to insure good drainage. Add soil, bark and larger stones. The children may want to shape the soil into hills and valleys.

Plant the larger plants first. Small ferns grow well. Cover the roots with soil. Leave space in between the plants. Spray to keep moist.

HOW DOES MOISTURE AFFECT GERMINATION?

YOU'LL NEED:

2 small glass bowls   seeds
gravel   soil

HERE'S HOW:

Line the bottom of one bowl with gravel. Put a layer of soil over the gravel. Put the seeds in the gravel, and water. Invert one bowl over the other. Expose the bowl to sun. Which seeds sprout first?

HOW DOES AIR AFFECT GERMINATION?

YOU'LL NEED:

lima bean seeds
radish seeds
4 jars

soil
cotton
water

HERE'S HOW:

Step 1: Plant bean seeds in first two jars. Fill one jar to the top with water so that air is forced out. Keep the temperature, light and water the same for both jars.

Step 2: Fill two other jars to the top with water. Place a cotton pad on the top. Place radish seeds on cotton to keep them moist. Drop seeds into water in the second jar, eliminating the air. Keep light and temperature the same for both jars.

Which seeds grew?
What conclusions can you make?
Is air essential to growth?

HOW DOES TEMPERATURE AFFECT GERMINATION?

YOU'LL NEED:

bean seeds
birdseed
3 flower pots
soil

cotton
3 cups
saucers

HERE'S HOW:

Step 1: Plant bean seeds in three flower pots and label them as shown:

Place "normal" pot at room temperature. Place "cold" in the refrigerator and "hot" near a heater vent.

Step 2: Place a pad of wet cotton in each of the three cups. Sprinkle birdseeds on each pad. Cover each cup with a saucer and label.

What happened to each pot?

What conclusions can we make about growth in warm, hot, cold areas?

TESTING SEEDS FOR GERMINATION

YOU'LL NEED:

yard of cotton flannel   100 radish seeds
pan of water   thermometer

HERE'S HOW:

Dampen flannel and place radish seeds on it. Roll loosely, placing one end in the pan of water. Put the thermometer in the pan, and place pan near an open window. Record temperature daily. After 10 days, unroll flannel and count the number of sprouted seeds.

Some seeds sprouted, others did not. Why?

What might increase germination?

HOW DO PLANTS GET THEIR FOOD?

YOU'LL NEED:

growing plants   celery stalks
red food coloring

HERE'S HOW:

Add food coloring to a glass of water. Then put the celery stalk into the glass of water. Watch what happens. Can you explain?

EXTRA! EXTRA!

1) Growing Bulletin Board

For each child place 3 or 4 lima bean seeds on a wet paper towel and put the towel into a bag. Tape the bag closed and print the child's name on the outside. Hang the bags on a bulletin board.

2) Seed Pictures

Give the children different seeds to trace and glue on paper.

3) Task Flowers

Give each child a paper cup. When he completes a task, note his accomplishment by encouraging him to make a flower for his cup.

4) Plants Grow — Can Chemicals Grow?

YOU'LL NEED:

glass bowl	charcoal
rocks	sponge pieces
jar	food coloring
6 Tbsp. water	6 Tbsp. salt
6 Tbsp. bluing	3 Tbsp. ammonia

HERE'S HOW:

Lightly wet the charcoal and sponge, and place them in the bowl. Mix chemicals in a jar, using only 3 Tbsp. salt. Pour mixture onto rocks, sponge and charcoal. Sprinkle food coloring and the second 3 Tbsp. salt evenly over the contents of the bowl. In a few hours you may see results.

What has formed? (crystals)

5) Nature Finds

YOU'LL NEED:

leaves   flowers
nuts   seeds

HERE'S HOW:

Take a walk to see what you can find.
> What did you find?
> What can you do with what you found?
> Can it grow? Find out.

6) What is a seed?

YOU'LL NEED:

3 beans   water
cup

HERE'S HOW:

Place beans in cup and cover with water. Allow to sit for twenty four hours.
> What are they like now?
> Are they larger than yesterday?
> Can you open them?
> What do you see inside the bean? Can you draw a picture?

7) Do Plants Need Sunshine?

YOU'LL NEED:

black construction paper   paper clips
growing plants with large leaves

HERE'S HOW:

Cut out a design from the black construction paper. Clip the design on the leaf and leave it for two days. Remove the construction paper and notice the results.
> What happened to the leaf? Why?
Draw a picture of the leaf before and after it was covered.

8) Grow a Sunflower

YOU'LL NEED:

seeds   container
soil   water

HERE'S HOW:

Fill the container with soil. Put two or three seeds in. Add a little more soil. Water. Wait and watch. Keep the seedlings in the light.

How many days before you see a leaf?
Which seed is bigger?
Which plant will be bigger?

9) Sets of Beans

YOU'LL NEED:

egg carton   jar of beans

HERE'S HOW:

Form sets of beans.

How are these beans alike?
How are these beans different?
How many different sets did you make?
Can you make other kinds of sets?

10) Grow a Bulb

YOU'LL NEED:

1 or more bulbs   pebbles or marbles
pie dish

HERE'S HOW:

Put the pebbles in the pie dish and add water. Put the bulbs in the middle of the dish. Water and wait 2 to 3 weeks.

A bulb carries its food inside. Will it grow without water?
Will it grow without air and light?

FOLLOW UP:

In the late fall, take your children outside. Give each child a bulb to plant. Talk about how each bulb looks, smells, and feels. Write an experience story. The results will bring joy to the children as they view their spring gardens.

11) Sorting Seeds

YOU'LL NEED:

container of seeds   egg carton

HERE'S HOW:

Place all seeds that are alike in one section of the egg carton. Use as many sections as needed.

How many different seeds do you think there are? Guess
In each section are the seeds the same size, color?
Can we grow each seed?
How many different sizes of seeds did you find?
How many different colors are there?

12) Photosynthesis

YOU'LL NEED:

box with windows in it   plant

HERE'S HOW:

Place box over plant.

How is the plant growing?
Is it growing straight?
Is it growing crooked?

13) A Story Garden

YOU'LL NEED:

plants with faces

HERE'S HOW:

Make up a story about what the plants are saying.

What is happening?
What could they be saying?

14) Who's Got the Beans?

YOU'LL NEED:

egg carton   pair of dice
bag of beans   plastic boxes (2" x 5" x 7")

HERE'S HOW:

Play the game and see who can get the most beans.
Rules:
1) Put the dice in the egg carton and shake.
2) Open carton and see what numbers you got.
3) Take that number of beans from the bag and put them in your box.
4) Person with most beans wins. (Can you subtract with this game?)

15) Terrarium

YOU'LL NEED:

large drinking glass   plants
pebbles   piece of glass
soil

HERE'S HOW:

Take a walk in the park or on school grounds. Collect small plants, moss, little stones. Put soil in the drinking glass and add the plants you collected. Water, then put the piece of glass on top. Watch it grow.

What will too much water do?
What will too little water do?
Does the terrarium need light?

16) Stems We Eat

YOU'LL NEED:

potatoes   carrots
onions   knife

HERE'S HOW:

Look at each stem. Cut one or two apart to see the inside. Eat a piece if you like.

Where is the food stored?
Where are the roots?
Where are the leaves?

17) Sorting: Plants We Eat — Plants We Don't Eat

YOU'LL NEED:

pictures of edible and nonedible plants

HERE'S HOW:

Look at each picture. Sort them out, making two piles: one pile for plants you can eat and one pile for plants you cannot eat.

Do you know all the edible plants?

Do you know the nonedible plants?

Resources and Children's Literature

Carle, Eric. *The Tiny Seed*. New York: Thomas J. Crowell Co., 1970.

Croft, Doreen and Robert Hess. *An Activities Handbook for Teachers of Young Children*. Atlanta, Ga.: Houghton Mifflin Co., 1976.

Fleming, Hamilton, and Hicks. *Resources for Creative Teaching in Early Childhood Education*. New York: Harcourt, Brace, Jovanovich, Inc., 1977.

Harlan, Jean D. *Science Experiences for the Early Childhood Years*. Columbus, Ohio: Charles Merrill Publishing Co.

Jordan, Helene. *How a Seed Grows*. New York: Thomas Crowell Co., 1970.

Krauss, Ruth. *The Carrot Seed*. New York: Scholastic Book Service.

Matawan School District Kindergarten Science Curriculum.

Russell, Helen Ross. *Ten Minute Field Trips: Using the School Grounds for Environmental Studies*. Chicago, Ill.: Ferguson, 1973.

Sholinksy, Jane. *Growing Plants from Fruits and Vegetables*. New York: Scholastic Book Services, 1974.

Sussex Chapter: The New Jersey Association for the Education of Young Children. *The Birds 'N the Bees*.

Chapter Four

L · I · G · H · T

How does light travel? Can I catch a sunbeam? Why does my shadow follow me? Children make observations about light and shadow early in their lives. The next two chapters help to answer their many questions and deal with natural and man-made light, refracted and reflected light, rainbows, mirrors, colors, infrared, and lenses. The children are encouraged to ask questions, observe, work with materials and draw conclusions. Enjoy their discoveries and guide their investigations. Let there be light!

Discovering & Exploring Light

SETTING UP A "LIGHT CENTER"

EQUIPMENT:

cardboard

straws

sheet

flashlight

mirrors

paper towel

can

glass

spoon

THINGS TO KNOW:

1) Light travels in a straight line.
2) Light can pass through some things and not through others.
3) Light can be natural or man-made.
4) Light can be reflected.
5) When light passes from one transparent material to another, rays are bent.
6) A lens is a transparent material.
7) Lenses are found in microscopes, binoculars, cameras.
8) A rainbow is a spectrum that is produced when sun shines through water.
9) Light rays can cause heat.

LIGHT TRAVELS

YOU'LL NEED:

3 cards

scissors

flashlight

pencil

ruler

clay

paper

HERE'S HOW:

Make a hole in the middle of each card. Stand them up in a row by imbedding them in the clay. Shine the flashlight through the holes and observe.

LIGHT AND SHADOW

YOU'LL NEED:

sheet	straws
light	tape
cardboard	scissors

HERE'S HOW:

Cut out a paper puppet and tape the straw to its back. Hang the sheet and place the light behind it. Put on a shadow play with the puppets.

SILHOUETTE

YOU'LL NEED:

light	paper
scissors	pencil

HERE'S HOW:

Have a friend sit between a wall and a light. Place the paper on the wall and trace your friend's outline. Cut it out and compare with others!

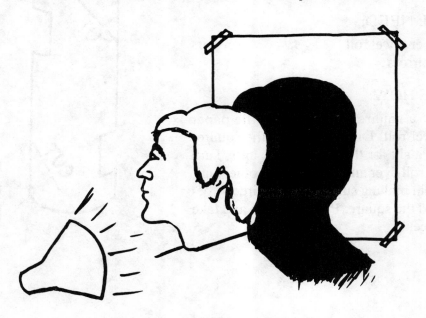

Light Chart

NATURAL	MAN-MADE
(sun)	(candle)
(stars)	(bulb)
(lightning bug)	(flashlight)

PERISCOPE

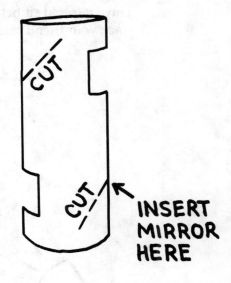

CUT

CUT

INSERT MIRROR HERE

YOU'LL NEED:

paper towel roll   scissors
2 mirrors

HERE'S HOW:

Cut a square in one end of the paper towel roll. Directly behind the square, cut a slit for the mirror to fit into. Turn the roll over and repeat at the other end, again making sure the slit is directly behind the square. Put mirrors in and take a peek!

REFRACTED LIGHT

YOU'LL NEED:

coin
pitcher

dish
water

HERE'S HOW:

Place a coin in a dish of water. Move the dish away until you cannot see the coin. Add water to the dish until the coin is visible.

MAKE A CAMERA

YOU'LL NEED:

soup can
elastic band

nail
waxed paper

HERE'S HOW:

Punch a hole in the bottom of the can. Cover the open end with waxed paper. Hold the can up with the waxed end facing you.

FOLLOW-UP:

1) Compare your tin can camera to a real camera.
2) Discuss the eye and its relation to the camera.
3) Flash a light into a friend's eye. What happens to the pupil of the eye?
4) Show how the eye is similar to a camera.

RAINBOWS

YOU'LL NEED:

prism
crayons
paper

sunlight
dish
water

HERE'S HOW:

Shine sunlight through a prism. Make a picture of what you see. Leave a dish of water on a sunlit shelf and observe what happens.

COLOR CHART

HERE'S HOW:

Chart the color of the shirts or blouses of your friends in the class

BLUE	YELLOW	RED	GREEN
JANET	TIM	BOBBY FRANK	SARA

HOW DO OBJECTS LOOK WHEN PLACED IN WATER?

YOU'LL NEED:

glass ruler
spoon water

HERE'S HOW:

Fill the glass two thirds full of water. Put the spoon in the glass of water. How does the spoon look? Draw a picture of what the spoon looks like in the glass.

Substitute a ruler and repeat the experiment. Draw a picture of what the ruler looks like in the water. Is there a difference between the ruler and spoon?

CAN YOU MAKE A MIRROR?

YOU'LL NEED:

glass
tape

black paper
lamp

HERE'S HOW:

Tape the black paper to one side of the glass. Turn on the lamp. Stand with your back to the lamp. Hold up the glass and look at it. What do you see?

HOW DO WE LOOK IN A MIRROR?

YOU'LL NEED:

a large mirror

HERE'S HOW:

Raise your left hand. Where does it appear in the mirror? Raise your right hand. Where does it appear in the mirror? What other things can you look at in the mirror?

WHAT CAN WE SEE IN A MIRROR?

YOU'LL NEED:

mirror

words on cards

HERE'S HOW:

Stand the mirror up behind the letters on the card. Can you read the words? Can you think of other words which can be read this way?

<u>YES</u>

DUUΛ (BOOK)

ᒐUUΝIᑕ (COOKIE)

UΠIᘜ (OHIO)

<u>NO</u>

ᒋUΙⱯΙ (FUNNY)

DᒐΛΠ (BEAR)

ΙⱯΙΙΠΠUΠ (MIRROR)

LIGHT SPOT TAG

YOU'LL NEED:

2 mirrors   partner

HERE'S HOW:

With a mirror, catch the light from the sun and reflect a "light" on the wall. With the second mirror, your partner tries to place a light spot on your spot. When he or she tags the spot with his or her "light," it becomes his or her turn the shine a spot on the ceiling for you to "tag."

WHAT DOES LIGHT PASS THROUGH?

YOU'LL NEED:

piece of glass   waxpaper
black paper   lamp

HERE'S HOW:

Turn on the lamp. Hold the glass between yourself and the lamp and look through it. Then try the waxpaper and the black paper. Which objects does the light pass through? Experiment with other objects. Make a chart of the objects which light passes through.

YES	NO
GLASS	BLACKPAPER

COLOR WHEEL

YOU'LL NEED:

white cardboard   string

blue, yellow, green, and red crayons

HERE'S HOW:

Cut out 2 circles 3" to 4" in diameter from white cardboard. Color half of one circle blue and the other half yellow; color one third of the other circle blue, one third green, and one third red. Punch two small holes near the center of both circles. Put the string through the holes and knot the ends. Twist the string, then stretch it out and let it spin. What color do you see as it spins?

INFRARED LIGHT

YOU'LL NEED:

shiny black can   dull black can
water   2 thermometers

HERE'S HOW:

Fill the cans with water. Put a thermometer in each can and set them both in sunlight. Take the temperature of the two cans every half hour for three hours and keep a record. What did you observe? Can you explain why?

HOW DOES LIGHT MAKE CHANGES?

YOU'LL NEED:

scissors   tape

black, red, yellow paper

HERE'S HOW:

Cut the paper in half. Place half the paper in a notebook and tape the other half on the window. Check the paper one week, two weeks, three weeks later. What changes did you see?

EXTRA! EXTRA!

1) Rainbow Crossword Puzzle

ACROSS
1) the name of a fruit (breakfast)
2) the color of the sky
3) apples are sometimes this color

DOWN
4) another name for purple
5) the color of grass
6) the color of a banana

L
I
G
H
T

2) Mixing Colors

Use finger paints to mix complimentary colors.
Use food coloring to experiment with colors. Show experiments on the overhead projector.

3) Heat with Sunlight

YOU'LL NEED:
mangnifying glass   paper
sunlight

HERE'S HOW:

Shine the sunlight on the paper through the magnifying glass.
Light rays produce heat — watch the paper smoke!

4) Make Your Own Crossword Puzzle

5) Word Scramble

HERE'S HOW:

Unscramble these words:

		Answer Key	
dowsha	ghlit	color	shadow
delcan	lrooc	opaque	candle
queapo	nseles	lenses	light

Light List

HERE'S HOW:

List all the words you can think of that have something to do with light:

color	dull
seeing	twilight
lighthouse	dark
candle	dawn
flashlight	hue
shade	colorful
bright	rainbow
shine	prism

71

Resources

Asimov, Isaac. *Light*. Chicago: LaFollet Publishing Co., 1970.

Beeler, *Experiment with Light*. New York: Crowell, 1957.

Branley, Franklyn, *What Makes Day and Night?* New York: Crowell, 1961.

Division of Curriculum Development, Board of Ed. of the City of New York. Science K-6, *Sound and Light in Communication, Book 4*. New York: Board of Education, 1965.

Epstein, Sam and Beryl. *Look in the Mirror*. New York: Holiday House, 1973.

Freeman, Ira. *All About Light and Radiation*. New York: Random House, 1965.

Harrison, George. *The First Book of Light*. New York: Watts, 1962.

Kohn, Bernice. *Light You Cannot See*. Englewood Cliffs, Prentice-Hall, 1965.

Meyer, Jerome S. *Prisms & Lenses*. Cleveland, Ind.: World Publishing Co., 1959.

Moore, Patrick. *Telescopes and Observatories*. New York: John Day Co., 1962.

Podendorf, Illa. *Color*. Chicago. Children's Press, 1971.

_____. *Shadows and More Shadows*. Chicago. Children's Press, n.d.

Simon, Seymour. *Let's Try it Out: Light and Dark*.

Free Materials

American Optometric Association, Inc., 4030 Chouteau Avenue, St. Louis 10, Missouri.

Bausch and Lomb Optical Company, 99360 Bausch Street, Rochester2, New York.

Diary Food and Nutrition Council, Inc. 172 Halstead Street, East Orange, N.J. 07018.

What We Do Day By Day
We All Need Milk — Animals Eat the 1, 2, 3 Way.

Dennison Mfg. Co., Framingham, Massachusetts.

Chapter Five

S · H · A · D · O · W · S

Shadows

I have a little shadow that goes
    in and out with me
And what can be the use of him is more
    than I can see.
He is very, very like me from the heels
    up to the head;
And I see him jump before me when I
    jump into my bed.
       From *My Shadow*
       Robert Louis Stevenson

Young children are fascinated by shadows although they do not understand them. They seem to appear and disappear for no apparent reason . . . is it magic? Eventually children may come to know that shadows appear with light, but that shadows appear differently in sunlight, moonlight, and fuel light.

Shadow play is enjoyable and amusing for children. You may want to try some of these activities on your own before sharing them with your children. Respect the willingness of the children to work. Some children will be content to know the different positions of a shadow and others will want to know why there is no shadow at all at a particular time.

Through exploration of shadows, children will be experimenting with spatial relationships in a simple but scientific way. This chapter's activities can be enjoyable as well as meaningful.

Discovering & Exploring Shadows

SETTING UP A "SHADOW CENTER"

EQUIPMENT:

cellophane
shoebox
flashlight

pins
lamp
sheet

THINGS TO KNOW:

1) We need light to make a shadow.
2) Shadow has no light.
3) Shadows change size.
4) Shadows move.
5) Shadows are formed when an opaque material is placed in the path of the light.

SHADOW DESIGN

YOU'LL NEED:

black paper
colored cellophane

straight pins

shoe box with an oval opening at one end to look through, an opening at the other end into which a flashlight will fit, and a slit on the top to insert the shadow design.

HERE'S HOW:

Punch out a design with the straight pins in the black paper. Place the paper in the box, insert the flashlight, and turn it on to see your design.

Tape colored cellophane to the back of the design and tape to the window.

PUPPET SHADOW PLAYS

YOU'LL NEED:

picture frame   glue
lamp   piece of bed sheet,
        cut to fit picture frame

HERE'S HOW:

Glue the piece of sheet to the
frame and put it on a table.
Place a lamp so that the light
shines on the "screen." Pup-
peteers kneel on the floor so
their shadows will not appear.
The puppets may be simple
outline drawings mounted on
sticks. Move the puppets between the light and the screen
to create a shadow play.

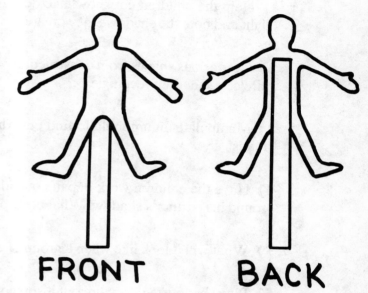

FRONT   BACK

Children may also cast shadows by standing between a hanging sheet and a
lamp.

FLASHLIGHT SONG
(Tune: "This Little Light of Mine")

HERE'S HOW:

Children sit in a circle with the lights off. Have children pass a small flashlight
around as they sing:

"This little light of   (child's name)   , s/he shines it on his/her
    (Wherever child shines light).

Repeat two times. End:

"This little light of   Mary's   , she shines it on her
    toe   , let it shine, let it shine!

EXTRA! EXTRA!

1) Help the children cut snowflake designs from construction paper. Hold them up to light and note the shadows they create.

2) Cut various shapes from construction paper. Note the shadow created by a triangle, a circle, a square, a rectangle.

3) Manipulate an umbrella to find out where its shadow is largest, smallest, roundest, fattest.

4) Have the children work in pairs outside. Give each child a piece of chalk to draw around his partner's shadow. What body parts show up in shadows?

5) What will it look like when a group of children put all their shadows together?

6) Play shadow tag. You are out if someone is able to step on your shadow.

7) Choose a pebble on the ground. Encircle it with the shadow of your hands.

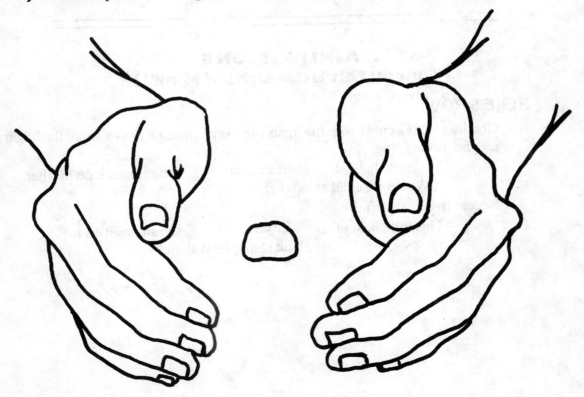

8) Stand with your shadow in front of you. Touch the head of your shadow. Hide your shadow.

9) Two partners try to touch shadow hands, fingers or shake shadow hands.

10) Draw a design on the blackboard such as / Use a flashlight to follow the chalk lines.

11) On a sunny window tape an X. Place an X on the wall each time the shadow moves.

Resources

Adler, Irving and Ruth. *Shadows*. New York: John Day Co., 1961.

Bulla, Clyde R. *What Makes a Shadow?* New York: Crowell, 1962.

deRegniers, Beatrice S. and Isabel Bordon. *The Shadow Book*. New York: Harcourt, Brace, Jovanovich, 1962.

Kranzer, Herman C. *Nature and Science Activities for Young Children*. Jenkingtown, Pa., Baker, 1969.

Chapter Six

M · A · G · N · E · T · S

The activities that follow are based on the properties of magnets. Before the children do specific tasks, they should first be encouraged to explore magnets and their properties on their own. For as Piaget says, "messing around" is a "form of active exploration and a response to spontaneous interests that serves a very important function in learning and development" (Wadsworth, p. 177).

It is possible that while "messing around," children may inadvertently perform some of these tasks. This is fine, expecially since such activity comes right from the child. We hope that when the children do perform these tasks, they will provoke probing questions in the children that can be used for the basis for further investigations.

Discovering & Exploring Magnets

SETTING UP A "MAGNET CENTER"

EQUIPMENT:

horseshoe

various metal objects

various non-metal objects

bar magnet

string

glass

THINGS TO KNOW:

1) Magnets attract some metals but not all.
2) Magnets may have different shapes.
3) Magnets sometimes attract each other and sometimes repel each other.
4) Permanent magnets can be used to make temporary magnets.
5) Magnets are strongest at their poles.

CARING FOR MAGNETS

1) Keep them away from heat.
2) Do not drop them.
3) Handle them with care.

FISHING WITH MAGNETS

YOU'LL NEED:

magnet

ruler for fishing pole

string

magnetic and nonmagnetic objects

HERE'S HOW:

Tie one end of a string to a magnet. Tie the other end of the string to a pole. Put various objects to fish for in a box, some magnetic, some nonmagnetic. What things attached to the magnet? What things did not attach to the magnet?

GUESS YOUR BEST

YOU'LL NEED:

yes chart
no chart
objects for
experimentation
magnet

HERE'S HOW:

Gather various materials in a box. Have children predict, test and then sort the things that will be attracted by the magnet and the things that will not be attracted. Place materials on the proper chart.

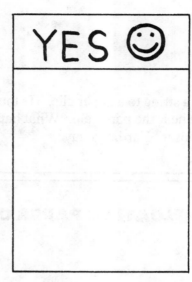

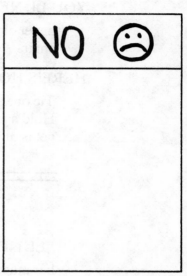

MAGNET MAGIC

YOU'LL NEED:

paper clips
a glass
a magnet
cardboard

wood
cloth
foil

HERE'S HOW:

1) Put some paper clips into a glass. Put a magnet beside the glass to see what happens.

2) Put an iron/steel object on a thin piece of cardboard. Place the magnet underneath the cardboard and watch what happens.

3) Do the same for wood, cloth, aluminum foil, material, or any other thin object.

FLYING PAPER CLIP

YOU'LL NEED:

paper clips   string
chair   magnet

HERE'S HOW:

Tie one end of a string to a paper clip. Tie the other end of the string to a chair. Hold a magnet near the paper clip. What happens? What happens if the magnet is moved closer? Farther away?

FLOATING PAPER CLIP

YOU'LL NEED:

bar magnet   paper clip
tack   string

HERE'S HOW:

Put a bar magnet on the top of a stand that looks like this so that it sticks off the edge. Put a tack into the bottom piece as shown. Tie a string to a paper clip. Wrap the other end of the string around the tack. Let the paper clip touch the magnet. Slowly pull the string away so the paper clip is not touching the magnet, but floats in the air. How far can the string be pulled before the paper clip does not float?

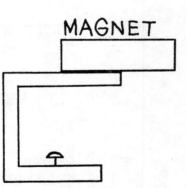

THIRSTY MAGNETS

YOU'LL NEED:

paper clips   glass of water
magnet

HERE'S HOW:

Put some paper clips into a glass. Fill the glass with water. Put the magnet into the water. What happens?

MAKE A MAGNET

YOU'LL NEED:

magnet   needle

pens or paper clips

HERE'S HOW:

Take a magnet and rub a needle on it (Rub one way only.) After rubbing for a while, use the needle to try to pick up some pins or paper clips. What has happened?

PICK UP STICKS

YOU'LL NEED:

magnets   nails

HERE'S HOW:

Lay some nails side by side without touching. Use a magnet to try to pick up one nail at a time without moving the other nails. Can it be done? Is there any other way to do it?

MIGHTY MAGNET

YOU'LL NEED:

bar magnet   paper clips
paper

HERE'S HOW:

To see where magnets are the strongest, spread out some paper clips on a piece of paper. Take a bar magnet and place it on the paper. Where did the clips go? Where is the magnet the strongest? (If appropriate, explain that the ends of the magnets are called the poles — north and south.)

MIGHTY, MIGHTY MAGNET

YOU'LL NEED:

magnet   iron filings

HERE'S HOW:

Another way to see where a magnet is the strongest is to put some iron filings on a paper. Then put a magnet under the paper and see where most of the filings go. Where is the magnet the strongest?

PUSHING AND PULLING MAGNETS

YOU'LL NEED:

2 bar magnets

HERE'S HOW:

Try to touch the two ends of two bar magnets together. What happens? Now turn the both magnets around and try again. What happens? Now turn around just one magnet. What happens?

MAGNET DOWELS

YOU'LL NEED:

wood block   drill
3 dowels   glue
                  8 magnets with holes in the center

HERE'S HOW:

Drill three holes in the wood block. Glue dowels in the holes. When thoroughly dry, slip magnets on each dowel. Children will explore attraction and repulsion as they experiment taking magnets off the dowels. Some magnets will be pulled together and others will push away.

MAGNET BOAT

YOU'LL NEED:

magnet   magnetized needle
piece of wood   water

HERE'S HOW:

Push the needle into the wood and place the wood in the water. Hold one pole of the magnet near the top of the needle. Then try the other pole. Which pole attracts the needle? Which pole repels the needle?

COMPASS

YOU'LL NEED:

magnetized needle   cork
sign hanging from ceiling: "Which direction is North?"
pan of water

HERE'S HOW:

Place the needle in the cork and put the cork into pan of water. Turn the cork in different directions. What happens each time you turn it?

MAGNETIC FOOTBALL

YOU'LL NEED:

Cardboard on which is drawn the design of a football field
2 strong magnets   a bottle cap

HERE'S HOW:

Each player has a magnet. The bottle cap is placed on the board. One opponent tries to "steal" the cap from the other and carry it to the goal line.

EXTRA! EXTRA!

1) Creative Writing

"If I had Magnetic Shoes . . ."

2) Watch This!

HERE'S HOW:

Place three large, strong circular magnets on a record turntable. Lower the top of the record player and cover it with smooth paper. Pour iron filings on the paper and turn the record player on. The filings play strange tricks. Ten penny nails are also fun to watch.

Resources

Adler, Irving and Ruth. *Magnets*. New York: The John Day Company, 1966.

Branley, Franklyn M. and Eleanor K. Vaughan. *Mickey's Magnet*. New York: Thomas Y. Crowell, 1956.

DeVito, Alfred. *Creative Sciencing*. Boston, Massachusetts: Little, Brown and Co., 1980.

Feravolo, Rocco. *Junior Science Book of Magnets*. Chicago, Ill.: Garrad Publishing Co., 1960.

Knight, David. *Let's Find Out About Magnets*. New York: Franklin Watts, Inc., 1967.

Lieberg, Owen. *Wonders of Magnets and Magnetism*. New York: Dodd, Mead and Co., 1967.

Podendorf, Illa. *Magnets and Electricity*. Chicago, Ill.: Children's Press, 1961.

Wadsworth, Barry J. *Piaget for the Classroom Teacher*. New York: Longman, Inc., 1978.

Yates, Raymond. *The Boys' Book of Magnetism*. New York: Harper and Row, 1959.

Chapter Seven

S · O · U · N · D

Sound is a form of energy produced by a vibrating object. It must have a medium through which to travel, such as air or other gases, liquids, or solids. It travels faster through substances with molecules close together and faster through warmer mediums than cold ones. Sound travels a mile in one second. The number of vibrations per second is called "frequency." The pitch of sound depends on the number of vibrations: the more vibrations, the higher the pitch. Loudness is measured by decibels, zero decibels representing a sound slightly fainter than that which a human ear can hear. An echo is a reflected sound. A musical sound is one whose wave patterns are regular. Noise is made by irregular patterns.

The ear is an important sense organ because in addition to hearing, the ear also gives the body a sense of balance. The outer ear is really a funnel which collects the sound vibrations and carries them into the middle ear, which is enclosed by a thin, tight sheet of tissue called the eardrum.

The sense of hearing is very important. It gives pleasure and can also warn of danger. Hearing is vital to communication, socialization, and intellectual and emotional development. Some children may have hearing disabilities. If a child repeatedly loses interest during story time or does not repsond readily to questions, he may have a hearing loss. It is important to discuss your observations with the child's parents as soon as possible.

Discovering & Exploring Sound

SETTING UP A "SOUND CENTER"

EQUIPMENT:

musical instruments

tuning fork

rubber bands

rulers

clock

pans

watches

THINGS TO KNOW:

1) We hear with our ears.
2) We listen to many sounds.
3) We learn many things by listening.
4) Sounds are made by things that vibrate. Sound consists of air vibrations that go into the ear.
5) Some people can't hear at all. They are deaf.
6) We can recognize some things by the sound they make: dogs, birds, motors, etc..
7) Sounds may be loud, soft, high, low, pleasant or harsh.
8) We need to take good care of our ears.

CAUTION: When presenting this concept, refrain from saying "Don't stick anything in your ears." Say, "We must keep our ears clean. We should be very careful not to hurt our ears, or the ears of anyone else."

VOCABULARY:

ear (s)

hear

deaf

talk

hum

sing

high/low

pleasant/harsh

tape recorder

telephone

sound

listen

vibration

whistle

whisper

shout

loud/soft

hearing aid

microphone

names of musical instruments

VIBRATIONS PRODUCE SOUND (I)

YOU'LL NEED:

12 inch ruler   table or desk

HERE'S HOW:

Lay a wooden ruler on a desk so that about 8" or 10" of the ruler extends over the edge. While holding the end of the ruler on the edge of the desk, press down hard on the free end and let go suddenly. What do you hear?

VIBRATIONS PRODUCE SOUND (II)

YOU'LL NEED:

rubber band   a box

HERE'S HOW:

Stretch the rubber band over the box. Pluck the rubber band. A humming sound is made by the band moving back and forth very quickly.

VIBRATIONS PRODUCE SOUND (III)

YOU'LL NEED:

a tuning fork   a pen
a pencil   a ruler

HERE'S HOW:

Hit prongs of tuning fork with a pen, pencil or ruler. Hold the fork near your ear. Then touch the fork prongs. The blow caused the fork prongs to vibrate and give off a humming sound. Touching the fork prongs stopped the sound.

FOLLOW UP:

Pluck a guitar, tap a drum, or place your hand on your throat (larynx) as you hum. Strike the tuning fork, listen to its sound, and then lower the prongs into a bowl of water and watch the water churn from these vibrations.

SOUND TRAVELS THROUGH THINGS (I)

YOU'LL NEED:

yardstick   clock
metal curtain rod

HERE'S HOW:

Have one child jump on the ground as another child places his ears to the ground and listens.

Have a child hold a yardstick to his ear. Hold a clock at the opposite end.

Have a child hold a metal curtain rod to his ear. Hold a clock at the opposite end.

The sounds will be heard more distinctly through the solid materials.

SOUND TRAVELS THROUGH THINGS (II)

YOU'LL NEED:

tin can or cardboard box   rice or any other grain
ruler

HERE'S HOW:

Put the grains in inverted can or box. Tap the can or box with ruler. The can will make a scratching sound as the grains hop up and down.

SOUND TRAVELS THROUGH THINGS (III)

YOU'LL NEED:

cottage cheese box   saran wrap
sugar or salt   paper

HERE'S HOW:

Cover box with saran wrap. Place sugar or salt on the saran wrap. Roll up paper like a megaphone and talk into it above the box. The salt or sugar will vibrate.

SEE	HEAR	TOUCH	SMELL	TASTE

SEASONAL SOUNDS

FALL	WINTER	SPRING	SUMMER

WHAT SOUNDS DID YOU HEAR ON OUR WALK?

LIZ	DOUG	SCOTT	PAT	TOM	SUE

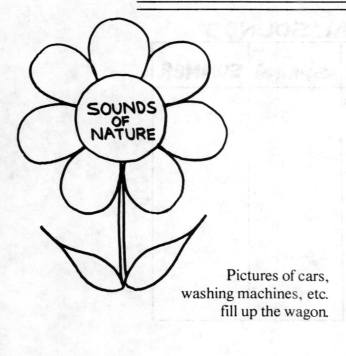

Each child can add a petal to this flower. Each petal has a nature sound on it.

Pictures of cars, washing machines, etc. fill up the wagon.

SOUND GAMES!

THINGS TO KNOW:

Children hear many sounds. Just hearing, however, does not mean listening. Listening involves recognizing sounds, giving them meaning from one's experience, reacting to or interpreting them, and integrating them with one's knowledge and experiences.

THE TELEPHONE

HERE'S HOW:

Thread a length of strong string through a hole in the bottom of each of two empty paper cups or tin cans. Now tie thick knots at the ends of the string so that they will not slip back through the holes. Give each cup to a child, and have them walk away from each other until the string is taut. Ask one to speak in a very low voice so that the other can barely hear him. Now ask him to speak in the same level of voice into his cup, while the other holds his cup to his ear. The listener will hear the voice more loudly, for the *string conducts sound better than air does.*

THE WATCH

HERE'S HOW:

Ask a child to stand at the opposite end of a bare table with a watch in his hand. You will hardly hear the ticking of the watch, if you hear it at all. Now, have the child place the watch on his end of the table while you ask several children to put their ears to the top of your end of the table. They will hear the watch ticking quite clearly. The table, which is solid, is a better sound-conductor than air.

93

THE TUBE

HERE'S HOW:

The children will enjoy playing with a cardboard tube from the inside of wrapping paper. Even though they may not understand the concept involved, they will have fun!

A child holds one end of the tube to his ear, while another child talks in a soft to moderate voice into the other end. The voice traveling through the tube is magnified. The children can also talk into a hat, with one child's ear inside, and hear the same magnification. In these instances, sound is *magnified; when it hits a solid object, it bounces back.*

NOTE: Have a discussion of the definition of the word "magnified." You may want to have a magnifying glass for the children's use. Stress that in these activities, our voices will be magnified, and we must not send a loud voice down the tube into someone's ear, as to do so could be harmful to the other child's eardrum.

SOUND CANS

YOU'LL NEED:

4 coffee cans of identical size, shape, and label	buttons
½ cup of sand	wood block
4 snap-on plastic lids	pieces of styrofoam

HERE'S HOW:

The children help fill the four cans so they can feel all the items, or they may reach into a can previously filled and try to guess what is inside. After the children have examined the cans, put a lid on each can, one at a time. When all the lids are on, shuffle the cans and have the children guess what is in each can by listening to them as they are shaken.

THINGS TO TALK ABOUT:

1) Comparison of weights
2) Comparison of sounds
3) Description of material — how it feels, how it sounds

VARIATIONS:

1) Make matching pairs of cans by filling each of two cans with the same material. Put a black lid on one and a yellow lid on the other. Make at least four pairs and mix them up. Match pairs by matching the sounds they make when shaken.
2) Children may place the cans in order from the loudest to the softest sound.

WHAT'S IN THE BOX?

YOU'LL NEED:

covered boxes   beans or buttons

HERE'S HOW:

Put a quantity of beans or buttons in each box. Children shake each box and guess how many beans or buttons are in it. Open the box and count to see if the child's guess was correct.

VARIATIONS:

Place in a box an object which makes a sound (whistle, bell, horn, etc.). Have children guess what's in the box and what sound it makes.

MUSIC, MUSIC, MUSIC

YOU'LL NEED:

rhythm band instruments

HERE'S HOW:

Put the instruments on table. Have children demonstrate the sounds made by each and correctly name the instrument.

Then have the children close their eyes and listen to one of the instruments making sounds. Ask one child to name the instrument. He then plays the next instrument for the children to identify.

THINGS TO TALK ABOUT:

1) Names of instruments being used.
2) How sounds are made — shaking, striking, etc.
3) Differences in pitch.

VARIATIONS:

Play "Same or Different?" The teacher, or one of the children, makes a sound with an instrument, pauses, and then plays either the same or a different instrument. Children say "Same" or "Different."

PAPER PLATE SHAKER

YOU'LL NEED:

paper plates
rice
macaroni

wide masking tape
beans

NOTE: You may also use any container that can be sealed and shaken easily — paper cups, tooth paste boxes, bandaid cans, etc.)

HERE'S HOW:

Enclose the various materials in between two paper plates stapled together or other containers as desired. Experiment with the different sounds the various materials make. Try the same material in different containers, or different materials in the same containers.

WOOD BLOCK TAMBOURINE

YOU'LL NEED:

scrap wood
nails with wide heads

bottle caps
hammer

bottle caps or tops of frozen juice containers (the ones removed by peeling a paper strip)

HERE'S HOW:

Teacher should prepare caps by punching hole in each with an extra wide nail. Children hammer the tops into the wood, using as many as they like to make tambourines. Experiment with the different sounds the bottle caps and juice tops make. If desired, let children paint their tambourines. You can use them at music time to beat out rhythms or to beat out a name: Jim-my, Jen-ni-fer.

SAND BLOCKS

YOU'LL NEED:

pine or any soft wood about 4" x 4" x 1½"
various textures of sandpaper
magic markers
scissors

thumbtacks
wooden spools
glue
hammer

HERE'S HOW:

Have the child sand his blocks with sandpaper. Then let him choose the texture of sandpaper he wants to use for his blocks. We have found that, if the teacher measures the piece needed, with supervision most children are able to cut the sandpaper using the teacher's scissors. Have the child wrap the sandpaper around one side of the block and fasten it with thumbtacks. Glue a wooden spool on the wooden side to be used as a handle. If desired, let children decorate the block with magic markers.

DRUM BEAT

YOU'LL NEED:

drum

HERE'S HOW:

Ask three children whose names contain a different number of syllables to stand before the group. (Example: Bob, Mary, Jennifer.) As the teacher taps one beat for each syllable on a drum, the children guess whose name she is tapping.

VARIATION:

As listening skill develops, last names can be used. The children will enjoy tapping each others' names.

BIG BANG, LITTLE BANG

YOU'LL NEED:

objects which may grossly differ in sound when dropped:
keys on a chain   a single key
a wooden block   a styrofoam block

HERE'S HOW:

Place several objects on the table and drop them one by one with the children watching. Then, the teacher closes her eyes and a child drops one object. The teacher guesses what has been dropped.

THINGS TO TALK ABOUT:

1) Soft and loud sounds in the room using comparative words — softer, softest, louder, loudest, etc.
2) Effect of height on sounds made.

FOLLOW UP:

Read *Shhh, Bang,* by Margaret Wise Brown, Harper and Row, 1943.

HIDE THE CLOCK

YOU'LL NEED:

loud clock or timer

HERE'S HOW:

Hide clock somewhere in the room. One child tries to locate it by its sound.

VARIATION:

Hide a button. Children clap to indicate how close the searching child is to the hidden object. Clap loudly when the searcher is close to the button and more softly the farther away he gets.

PARROT TALK

YOU'LL NEED:

2 paper bag puppets   a parrot and some other such as an owl

HERE'S HOW:

Teacher discusses with the children that parrots like to repeat everything they hear. The teacher says something and asks the class to repeat it like parrots.

For example:

Teacher: Good morning!
Class: Good morning!
Teacher: How are you?
Class: How are you? etc.

Introduce the two paper bag puppets. Teacher is the owl and he selects a child to be the parrot. Two of the children may play the game also.

THINGS TO TALK ABOUT:

Childrens' own experiences with talking birds. Focus children's listening on inflections in teacher's voice.

BASKET GAME

YOU'LL NEED:

basket with one article for each child.

HERE'S HOW:

Distribute the articles. Play a directions game with such instructions as, "Whoever has a pink flower, hop up to the basket and put it in." Vary the directions with hop, skip, jump, etc.

Many young children come to the school situation without the necessary experiential background upon which language must be based. They may have been in a limited world, meager in the ingredients that stimulate curiousity. When children come to school without this essential background, the teacher's role of providing the necessary experiential enrichment is very important.

THE SOUND CENTER!

Older children will enjoy a Sound Center. Provide them with materials and task cards so that they may proceed on their own.

task card #1

YOU'LL NEED:

cassette tape recorder
your science log book
pictures of objects which make sounds

tape of *Familiar Sounds*
pencil or pen

HERE'S HOW:

Listen to the tape alone. Try to identify the sounds you hear by writing them in your log book. Don't worry about spelling. Now listen to the tape again using the pictures in the box where the tape was started.

THINK:

Were most of the sounds familiar to you? What sounds were the easiest to recognize? the hardest?

RECORD:

1) The sounds you recognized on the tape.
2) Your answers to the *think* questions.

task card #2

YOU'LL NEED:

ruler

cake spatula

HERE'S HOW:

Hold the ruler on your work table. Let part of the ruler stick out over the edge. Hold the part on the table down with one of your hands or a heavy book. Hit the free end of the ruler with your other hand and listen to the sound the ruler makes. Do the same thing with the cake spatula.

THINK:

Does the ruler make a high sound or a low sound? Does the spatula make the same kind of sound as the ruler? What happens if you move the ruler along the table? Does it always sound the same?

RECORD:

Write down the answers to the *think questions* in your science log book.

task card #3

YOU'LL NEED:

a partner
rubber bands

magic marker
pad of manila newsprint paper

HERE'S HOW:

Set up a ruler on your worktable as you did for Task Card #2. Revove the top from the magic marker and attach it perpendicularly to the free end of the ruler. Have your partner hold the pad of newsprint next to the marker so that the writing end of the marker is touching the paper. Bend the ruler down and let go. The marker should make "waves" on the paper. Move the ruler up and down the table and repeat the experiment.

THINK:

Were all the "waves" alike? When did you get the longest waves? The shortest?

RECORD:

Draw a diagram of how you attached the marker to the ruler in your science log book. Tape your sound wave pictures to the wall.

---

task card #4

YOU'LL NEED:

a partner
pen or pencil

paper

HERE'S HOW:

Write down all the different sounds you hear around you (Examples: Whack! Ping! Clunk!)

THINK:

How many different sounds can you and your partner think of?

RECORD:

Please staple your list to the inside cover of your science log book.

task card #5

YOU'LL NEED:

scissors   glue
construction paper   magazine

HERE'S HOW:

Make a sound collage! Cut pictures from the magazines that show people, animals or things making sounds. You may include words that spell sounds.

THINK:

Lots of things make sounds, but can you always tell what kinds of sounds they make by looking at a picture?

RECORD:

Put your finished collage on the bulletin board. Please remember to put your name on the back of your collage.

task card #6

YOU'LL NEED:

How You Talk by Paul Showers   balloons

HERE'S HOW:

Read the story. Turn to page 16 in *How You Talk*. Follow the directions for making a balloon larynx.

THINK:

Can you make the same kind of noises the balloon makes?

RECORD:

Write down in your science log book the number of times you made your balloon larynx. Also write down the definition of larynx in your log book.

task card #7

YOU'LL NEED:

large empty bottle   pitcher of water

HERE'S HOW:

Fill bottle with water slowly.

THINK:

Listen to the different sounds made when the bottle is being filled up with water.

RECORD:

What different kinds of sounds did you hear? When did the sound change? Record your answer in your log.

task card #8

YOU'LL NEED:

tin cans   rope
friend

HERE'S HOW:

Make a tin can telephone and use it with your friend.

THINK:

What helped you to hear your friend's voice?

RECORD:

Write in your science log the answer to the think question. Look up the word "conduction" and add this to your list in your dictionary.

task card #9

YOU'LL NEED:

6 glasses the same size

HERE'S HOW:

Pour different amounts of water in each. Hit the glasses softly with a spoon. Put the glasses in order from the lowest to the highest pitch.

THINK:

Which will have the lowest pitch? Which will have the highest pitch?

RECORD:

Draw a picture in your log of the glasses going from lowest to highest pitch. Color the levels in each glass with a crayon. Why do you think some are low-pitched and some are high-pitched?

task card #10

YOU'LL NEED:

5 bottles with water in them   ruler

HERE'S HOW:

Blow into bottles to find the different pitches. Put the bottles in order from lowest to highest.

THINK:

Which do you think will have the lowest pitch? Which do you think will have the highest pitch?

RECORD:

Is there anything else in the bottles besides water? Measure the air column in each bottle and record it in your log. Do you see any relationship between the air columns and pitch?

task card #11

YOU'LL NEED:

set of bells of different sizes

HERE'S HOW:

Ring 2 bells at a time and tell which one is lower and which is higher. Put all the bells in order of lowest to highest.

THINK:

Do you think any of the bells will sound the same? How many do you think will have different sounds?

RECORD:

Answer think questions in your log. Draw the bells in your log book, showing them from the lowest to the highest sound. What can you tell about sound, looking at the pictures you drew and the bells you put in order from highest to lowest?

task card #12

YOU'LL NEED:

bamboo

HERE'S HOW:

Blow over the open end of each piece of bamboo and arrange them from the lowest to the highest.

THINK:

What made the pitch change? Can you remember another task you did that showed high and low pitches?

RECORD:

Answer think question. What can you tell about the lengths and pitches of sound? What do you think would happen if you put clay down the bamboo tubes? Would it change their pitches?

task card #13

YOU'LL NEED:

    construction paper   scissors
    tape

HERE'S HOW:

Make a paper cone, secure it with tape and cut off the pointed end. Listen to the sounds in the room both with and without the cone. Also listen while cupping your hand around your ear.

task card #14

YOU'LL NEED:

    guitar

HERE'S HOW:

Make as many different kinds of sounds with the guitar as you can: pluck, strum, press.

THINK:

How can you make the sound higher? Lower? Can you state a relationship between length and/or thickness of strings and the sounds they produce?

task card #15

YOU'LL NEED:

record player
paper cone with pin inserted through end

78 rpm record

HERE'S HOW:

Play the record using the pin and cone instead of the needle. Examine the grooves.

THINK:

What did you feel through the cone as the record played? How does a record make sound?

task card #16

YOU'LL NEED:

tub
2 rocks

water

HERE'S HOW:

Produce sound using the rocks, both in and out of water.

THINK:

How does water affect sound? Why should we not tap on the glass of a fish tank?

task card #17

YOU'LL NEED:

broomstick
partner

watch

HERE'S HOW:

Listen to the watch through the brommstick. Listen again without the stick between your ear and the watch.

THINK:

Which medium, air or wood, is a better conductor of sound? Why do you think this is? How else can you test your answer?

task card #18

YOU'LL NEED:

box of small cans, each with different materials

HERE'S HOW:

Match the cans by sound. Predict what they contain.

THINK:

Which contents make the most distinctive sounds and so were easier to guess? What was it that made them easier? Does the type of container affect the sound you can hear?

task card #19

YOU'LL NEED:

blindfold   partner

HERE'S HOW:

Have your blindfolded partner locate you by the sounds you make (clapping, speaking, etc.)

THINK:

How do ears help us tell the distance and direction of sound? How good are they?

---

task card #20

YOU'LL NEED:

2 funnel tubes
blindfold   partner

HERE'S HOW:

Blindfold your partner and reverse his or her sense of directions through hearing by putting the narrow end of a funnel to one ear and the wide end of the second funnel to the other ear.

THINK:

How do you use ears to tell direction? If you suddenly began to hear "backwards" like this, would it be hard to do things like walking? Why? Would it be hard to get used to?

task card #21

YOU'LL NEED:

The True Book of Sounds We Hear by Illa Podendorf

HERE'S HOW:

Read the book.

THINK:

How important is sound? How do we sort out all the sounds we hear at once, so we can hear what we want to? Write about how it would be to be deaf.

task card #22

YOU'LL NEED:

funnel tube   watch

HERE'S HOW:

Find the least distance from which you can hear the watch without the tube. Using the tube, find the greatest distance from which you can hear it.

THINK:

What does this tube do to help you hear? What is the name of this instrument and what uses can you find for it?

EXTRA! EXTRA!

Listening for Sounds in the Environment

1) Read *The Listening Walk*, by Paul Showers. Thomas Crowell, New York, 1961. Take the class on a listening walk, and have the children identify the various sounds.

When you return to the classroom, make a picture graph of the sounds that the children heard. Under each picture list the names of the children who heard the sound.

Make a chart to classify sounds of nature/man-made sounds.

This activity also teaches the skills for collecting information, sharing information, and recording information.

2) Arrange a "sound" table; display objects that make different sounds such as a bell, horn, drum, whistle, etc.

3) Play a tape of previously recorded sounds from their environment to see if the children can identify them.

4) Make popcorn, emphasizing the *sound*.
  Learn the song:
> "Jimmy pops corn, and I don't care,
> I'm popping right up in the air,
> I'm popping up and I'm popping down,
> and I'm popping all around the town!"
>> *Tune:* "Jimmy Cracked Corn"

5) Have children cut out pictures of things that make sounds from magazines to make a large collage.

6) If possible, take a trip to a real farm or zoo to provide a firsthand experience for the group.
  Make charts:
> "Animal Sounds on the Farm"
> "Other Sounds on the Farm"

Sing "Old MacDonald's Farm," mounting pictures of the animals mentioned on a flannelboard to give a visual picture to the younger children.

Make animal dominoes with oaktag and animal stickers, having the children match the animals that make the same sound.

For younger children, provide large flashcards with animal pictures cut out from old storybooks. Have children make the animal sounds as you flash the cards.

7) Play "What's Going On?"

Record children with a tape recorder talking or singing and then play the tape back to them.

Record play time and have children listen for clues to decide what was happening.

Discuss loud and soft sounds, heavy and light treads, fast and slow pace, and different sounds at home and at school.

Make a chart: "Home and School Sounds."

What are the "Sounds of Weather?" (Example: rain, thunder, hail, etc.)

Talk about the sounds of the seasons. Start a chart of the Fall season, leaving spaces for the other seasons. Add to the chart as the seasons change.

Relates sounds to holidays, such as bells for Christmas, a turkey's gobbling for Thanksgiving, a scary sound for Halloween. Discuss the sounds the children like.

Talk about "Happy Sounds" or "Sad Sounds." What are they?

These activities take the children from the concrete sounds around them to the more abstract concept of recalling sounds from past experiences.

8) Play "Which Made the Sound?"

You will need coffee can with plastic cover, teaspoon, cotton, button and crayon. One at a time, put each item in the coffee can and shake it so that children hear the sounds each item makes when it is shaken inside the can. Then have the children cover their eyes while one child chooses an item, puts it in the can and shakes it. Have the children guess which item is inside the can.

9) Another version of "Which Made the Sound?"

You will need a table, empty glass, a pitcher containing water, scissors, paper, bell, rhythm sticks, or other sound-producing items which the children are familiar with in the classroom. Put all items on the table.

Seat children with their backs to the table. Do an activity which produces sound, such as cutting paper with scissors, etc. Have children guess what made the sound.

10) Play "Can You Guess?"

Children close their eyes. Choose one child to do an activity which produces noise (examples: running, jumping, click tongue, snap fingers, hum, etc.). Other children guess what the child is doing.

NOTE: With young children, it would be a good idea to have the group do many of the activities in preparation for each doing it alone. A good question would be, "Who can think of sounds we can make by using our own bodies?"

11) Play "Watch and Listen"

You will need a metal tray, penny, rubber ball.

Children watch and listen as you drop the penny and rubber ball onto the tray. Then have the children close their eyes while you drop the articles one at a time onto the tray. Ask: "Which sound did you hear first, the ball or the penny?"

This activity requires children to listen for the sound before giving an answer.

12) The Teletrainer

The Telephone Company will provide your school with a Teletrainer to use for a few days. The accompanying filmstrips and materials are not suitable for young children, but the Teletrainer is great fun. It consists of two activated telephones and a loudspeaker unit which provide dial tone, ringing, and busy signals. The children may actually talk to each other over these phones, and dial their numbers if they are able to with the teachers' help if necessary.

After this "practice," we allow the children to use our real telephone to dial home and talk to their mother.

Children's Books for Listening and Sound

Aliki. *My Five Senses*. New York: Crowell, 1962.

Austin, Margot. *Growl Bear*. New York: Dutton, 1951.

Baruch, Dorothy. *Pitter Patter*. Wm. Scott, 1943.

Bendick, Jeanne. *The Human Senses*. New York: Watts, 1968.

Borton, Helen. *Do You Hear What I Hear?* New York: Abelhard, 1960.

Brandey, Franklyn. *Rusty Rings a Bell*. New York: Crowell, 1957.

Brown, Margaret Wise. *SHH — Bang!* . New York: Harper and Row, 1943.

_____. *The Noisy Books (Country, Indoor, Quiet, Seashore, Summer, Winter)*. New York: Harper and Row, 1940.

Carlson, Bernice. *Listen! And Help Tell the Story*. New York: Abingdon Press, 1965.

Dawson, Rosemary. *A Walk in the City*. New York: Viking Press, 1950.

Emberley, Ed. *Cock-A-Doodle-Do*. New York: Little, Brown and Company, 1964.

Flack, Marjorie. *Ask Mr. Bear*. New York: Macmillan, 1932.

Garelick, Mary. *Sounds of a Summer Night*. New York: Young Scott, 1963.

Galdone, Paul. *It Does Not Say Meow*. New York: Seabury, 1972.

Grifalconi, Ann. *City Rythms*. Indianapolis, Inc.: Bobbs Merrill, 1965.

Harvath, Betty. *The Cheerful Quiet*. New York: Watts, 1969./

Hutchins, Pat. *Goodnight, Owl*. New York: Mcamillan, 1972.

Keats, Ezra Jack. *Whistle for Willie*. New York: Viking, 1964.

MacPherson, Elizabeth. *The Wonderful Whistle*. New York: Putnam, 1965.

McGovern, Ann. *Too Much Noise*. New York: Houghton Mifflin, 1967.

Nelson, Lee. *All The Sounds We Hear*. Steck, 1960.

Shower, Paul. *The Listening Walk*. New York: Crowell, 1961.

Skarr, Grace. *What Do the Animals Say?* New York: Doubleday, 1972.

Spier, Peter. *Crash! Bang! Boom!* New York: Doubleday, 1972.

Steiner, Charlotte. *Listen to My Seashell*. New York: Knopf, 1959.

Tresselt, Alvin. *Rain Drop Splash*. Boston, Massachusetts: Lothrop, 1962.

Weir, R.C. *The Great Big Noise*. Chicago, Illinois: Follet, 1948.

Wells, Rosemary. *Noisy Nora*. New York: Dial Press, 1973.

Records

Creative Rhythms for Children Series. — Phoevbe James (good Indian dance and drum beats)

Hear and Tell. — Happy House Record C-21, Haddon Record Corp.

Let's Have a Parade. — Happy House Record C-39, Haddon Record Corp.

Little Brass Bank. — Young People's Records.

Muffing and Mother Goose. — Young People's Records.

My Five Senses. — Thomas Crowell.

Noisy and Quiet. Tom Glazer, RCA Camden.

Out-Of-Doors. — Young People's Records.

Rhythm Time: Mechanical Rhythms. — Bowmar Records.

Sounds Around Us. — (3 record album) Scott Foresman Co.

The Listening Walk. — Thomas Crowell.

Recognition of "sounds" in classical or semi-classical music:

Animals — *Peter and the Wolf,* Prokofiev.

Bee — *Flight of the Bumble Bee,* Rimsky-Korsikoff.

Bells — *1812 Overture,* Tchaikovsky – Mercury Record MC 50054.

Cannon — *1812 Overture,* Tchaikovsky.

Donkey — *On the Trail* from *Grand Canyon Suite,* Ferde Grofe.

Footsteps — *1812 Overture,* Tchaikovsky.

Clock — *The Clock Symphony,* Haydn.

Rain — *Little April Shower,* from "Bambi."

> All records and songs are appropriate for listening to "sound." Use favorites to point out high sounds, low sounds, loud and soft sounds, fast and slow tempos, rhythms and moods.
>
> Excellent records for listening and moving with the interpretation of music include:

Major Classics for Minors — RCA Victor LBY-1016
>   Side 1 – Variety of tempos for interpretive dancing.
>   Side 2 – *Wedding March from Lohengrin: Clowns* — Prokoviev.

Dreamy — *Liebestraum,* Liszt.

March — *March Militaire,* Schubert.

Spooky — *In the Hall of the Mountain King,* from *Peer Gynt Suite,* Grieg.

Kingly — *Pomp and Circumstance,* Elgar.

Happy — *Traumerei,* Schumann.

Resources

Carlson, Bernice Wells. *Listen! And Help Tell the Story.* New York: Abingdon Press, 1965.

Carmichael, Viola S. *Science Experiences for Young Children.* Cal.: Southern California Association for the Education of Young Children, 1969.

Collier, Mary Jo. *Kids' Stuff*. Cal.: Acoustifone Corp., 1969.

Dawson, Mildred. *Learning to Listen*. New York: World Book, 1962.

Engle, Rose C. *Language Motivating Experiences for Young Children*. Cal.: DFA Publishers, 1969.

Kranzer, Dr. Herman. *Nature and Science Activities for Young Children*. Pa.: Baker Publishers, 1969.

McGavack, John. *Guppies, Bubbles, and Vibrating Objects*. New York: John Day and Co., 1969.

Munson, Howard R. *Science with Simple Things*. Cal.: Fearon Publishing, 1972.

Platts, Mary E. *Launch*. Mich.: Educational Service, Inc., 1972.

Reid, Robert W. *Science Experiments for the Primary Grades*. Cal.: Fearon Publishers, 1972.

Wagner, et. al. *Science Games and Activities*. New York: Macmillan Co., 1973.

Free Material

N.J. Bell Telephone Company
(Contact your local office)
(A Program Planner is available which lists a variety of programs and films.)

American Telephone and Telegraph
195 Broadway
New York, New York

General Motors Corporation
Education Relations Section
P.O. Box 177 North End Station

Science Research Association
52 West Grand Avenue
Chicago 10, Illinois

Sound and Noise
Motor Vehicle Manufacturers' Association of the United States, Inc.
3001 New Center Building
Detroit, Michigan   48202
Undated. — 14 pp. Free.
A color illustrated booklet to acquaint the reader with the general principles of sound. Contains glossary.

Dear Parents:

At school we have been talking about sounds. I hope you will extend your child's vocabulary by continuing this study at home.

Here are some suggestions for ways to help. You will think of others as you work and play together.

1) Listen to and discuss the sounds which wake you in the morning.

2) Listen to and discuss sounds around the house. For example, the sounds of the washing machine, dishwasher, water dripping, etc.

3) When straightening up the child's room, as the two of you pick up toys, talk about the kinds of sounds the toys make (loud, soft). Talk about how the sounds are made (shake, hit, etc.).

4) Look through magazines and find pictures of things which make sounds.

Sincerely,

Teacher's Name

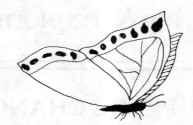

Chapter Eight

C·H·A·N·G·E·S

Leaves turn colors every fall. A caterpillar spins a chrysalis and becomes a butterfly.

Changes in our environment are taking place all the time. Young children can observe these changes and note the results. When changes occur, new materials are made that are entirely different from those elements that went into the process.

To begin observation and experimentation with changes, discuss the meaning of change. "Can you name something that changes?" Ask the children to bring, in a closed container, something they think will change. "Can you *predict* what changes may occur?"

The activities in this chapter deal with natural changes in the environment and encourage the children to observe, form hypotheses, and experiment to test each hypothesis. Young children are capable of recording results, developing ideas about why things happen, and trying things out to see "what happens if..."

The teacher directs, assists and helps the young child develop skills that will aid his investigations and research. The activities suggested here are designed to draw on resources within the child's environment, and encourage independent participation on the part of the child.

Discovering & Exploring Change

SETTING UP "THE CHANGE CENTER"

EQUIPMENT:

art supplies   clock

balloons   straws

bottle   clay

THINGS TO KNOW:

1) Change means "to become different."
2) There are *chemical* and *physical* changes.
3) Changes occur in many different ways.
4) Some changes are reversible, some are irreversible.
5) Some chemical changes are desirable, some are not.

CREATE A CHANGE

YOU'LL NEED:

crayons   glue

construction paper

     collected materials (leaves, paper or fabric scraps)

HERE'S HOW:

Draw a picture and glue your collected materials to it. Hang your picture near sunlight. What do you think will happen? Which things will change? Look at your picture each day. Can you see the changes?

BALLOONS (I)

YOU'LL NEED:

balloons   paper clips

tape

HERE'S HOW:

Blow up your balloon and fasten the paper clip to the end. Tape the balloon to the bulletin board. Observe it during the day. What changes do you see?

BALLOONS (II)

YOU'LL NEED:

1 long balloon   1 round balloon

HERE'S HOW:

Discuss the size and shape of the balloons with a friend. Each of you take one balloon and blow it up. Which balloon was filled first? How did each balloon's size and shape change?

BALLOONS (III)

YOU'LL NEED:

balloons   markers

HERE'S HOW:

Draw a design on your balloon. Blow it up. How did your picture change?

BALLOONS (IV)

YOU'LL NEED:

bottle   balloon

HERE'S HOW:

Put the balloon over the bottle. Set the bottle in a warm place. Watch this change take place.

121

REVERSIBLE CHANGES

YOU'LL NEED:

2 balls of red clay   2 balls of yellow clay

HERE'S HOW:

Mix a yellow ball and a red ball together. What color do you see? Can you make one ball *all* red again?

SUNLIGHT AND REFRIGERATION

YOU'LL NEED:

milk   2 clear glasses
plastic wrap   marking pencil
chart paper

HERE'S HOW:

Shake the milk and pour equal amounts into each glass. Mark the levels with the marking pencil and cover with plastic wrap. What will happen if you put one glass in the refrigerator and one in sunlight? Record these changes. (The milk curdles.)

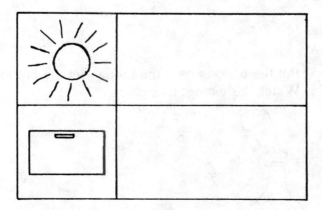

MELTING AND FREEZING (I)

YOU'LL NEED:

2 containers   ice cubes
clock

HERE'S HOW:

Put one ice cube in each container. Place one container in the freezer and the other on a shelf for observation. What happens? Can you time the melting process?

MELTING AND FREEZING (II)

YOU'LL NEED:

1 ice cube for each child   stop watch or clock

HERE'S HOW:

Who can melt his ice cube first? How many ways can you make the ice cube melt?

Make this chart:

	METHOD
1st cube to melt ___ min.___ sec. 2nd cube to melt ___ min.___ sec.	

WATER DROPLETS

YOU'LL NEED:

straw   water

HERE'S HOW:

Fill the straw with water and hold your finger over the end. Let a small droplet come out. Observe.

Now add detergent to the water. Fill the straw again and let some droplets fall. Were the water droplets easier to make? What can you say about their size and shape?

FOOD COLORING (1)

YOU'LL NEED:

craft stick   food coloring
water   glasses

HERE'S HOW:

Fill the glasses with water, and then add 2 drops of food coloring. Use craft stick to stir. What do you see? Mix all colors.

Use 4 different colors and follow the same directions.

Place one glass in front of the other and look through them both. What do you see? Hold a glass up to the light. Can you think of other ways to change the colors?

R = RED
Y = YELLOW
B = BLUE

R + Y = ?
B + R = ?
Y + B = ?

SOUND (I)

YOU'LL NEED:

rubber bands of different sizes

HERE'S HOW:

Stretch the rubber band. How does it look? Pluck it. How does it sound? How does a thin rubber band sound compared with a thicker one? Can you think of a musical instrument that sounds like the rubber band? What is it?

SOUND (II)

YOU'LL NEED:

spoon   water
4 glasses

HERE'S HOW:

Tap each glass with spoon. Do they sound alike? Blow across the tops. Can you hear a sound? Now fill the glasses with water, each at a different level.

Blow across the tops. Notice the new sound. Tap with a spoon. Which sounds are high? Low?

RUST
(A chemical change)

YOU'LL NEED:

2 large iron nails   house paint
water   jar with cover

HERE'S HOW:

Paint one nail and stand both nails in a jar containing a small amount of water. Cover and let it stand. What do you notice after a few days? Oxygen from the air has united with the iron in the unpainted nail to make the iron rust. Scrape off the rust and you will see that the nail no longer looks like iron. What kept the other nail from rusting?

SUGAR

YOU'LL NEED:

½ tsp. sugar   pan
heat

HERE'S HOW:

Heat sugar until it has turned black. Let cool and taste. What new material has formed?

DISSOLVING POWDERS

YOU'LL NEED:

spoon   glass
water   sugar or salt

HERE'S HOW:

Add sugar or salt to warm water. What happens? Sitr. Watch the changes. Do you see the water evaporate and change to crystal from? Add some food coloring to the water and repeat the experiment.

PRODUCING CARBON DIOXIDE

YOU'LL NEED:

1 to 2 tsp. baking soda   3 Tsp. vinegar
match

HERE'S HOW:

Pour vinegar on baking soda and observe. Hold a match over the bubbles. What happens to the match? How could this idea be put to use?

WOOD

YOU'LL NEED:

blocks of wood   sandpaper

HERE'S HOW:

Sand the wood. What changes do you see?

EXTRA! EXTRA!

1) Bake Bread — What chemical changes do you see?

2) Place mothballs in water. What happens? Strain the water through cheese cloth. What remains?

3) Mold Garden — Place bread, lettuce, orange, and egg in a glass bowl near a window. Mold will begin to grow. Are all molds the same? Which items develop mold first? Last?

4) Drying — Place mud, paint and clay in separate containers. Which dries out first? Place another set in the refrigerator. Is the drying out time the same?

5) Make a list of objects that rust.

6) Fill in: When ice _____ it becomes water.
When you blow into a balloon it becomes _____ .

7) Sequence shots – Draw pictures of:
1) A seed progressing through the stages of growth.
2) A town and tree under bright sun, slowly drying out.
3) A melting snowman as the sun rises.
Then cut the pictures apart, mix them up and put them back into correct sequence.

Resources

Croft, Doreen J. and Robert D. Hess. *An Activities Handbook for Teachers of Young Children*. Hoepwell, N.J.: Houghton Mifflin, 1975.

Nelson, Leslie W. and George C. Lorbeer. *Science Activities for Elementary Children*. Dubuque, Iowa: Wm. C. Brown Co., 1972.

Free Materials

Sample Packet of Teaching Aids.
DelMonte Teaching Aids.
P.O. Box 9075
Clinton, Iowa 52732
Single packets free. Allow 6-8 weeks for delivery. Several guides, kits, wallcharts, recipe booklets are available at nominal costs. Send for listing.

Chapter Nine

E·L·E·C·T·R·I·C·I·T·Y

Batteries, bulbs, circuits and fuses — too difficult for young children? Not at all! Exploration of electricity should be done in a manner that insures the safety of young children. Flashlight and battery activities will not produce enough power to harm the participants.

You will experience a sense of joy and accomplishment when your students successfully complete any experiment. There always seems to be a special satisfaction in making a bulb light with only the minimum equipment. Remember also, that your students do not have to know and understand the reasons why something happens the way it does. It is important that they develop an awareness of electricity and have the opportunity for "hands-on" experiences.

Even though they were not always aware of it, all children have had experiences with electricity. This chapter incorporates activities to delight the very young, as well as to challenge the older students through independent center work and **Task Cards.** After completing these activities, children will better understand why they often receive a shock while running across the carpet!

Discovering & Exploring Electricity

SETTING UP AN "ELECTRICITY CENTER"

EQUIPMENT:

dry cell	bells
sockets	nails
light bulbs	batteries
wire	circuit box

THINGS TO KNOW:

1) Identify causes of static electricity, including meaning and use of following terms: friction, charge (negative and positive), conductor.

2) Identify "evidence of interaction" in operating electric circuits.

3) Identify open and closed circuits.

4) Make children aware of the importance electricity plays in their lives.

5) Recognize dangers of electricity.

MAKING ELECTRIC SPARKS
(Static electricity can by made by rubbing)

YOU'LL NEED:

    sheet of paper   sheet of plastic

HERE'S HOW:

    Place a sheet of paper on your desk. Put a sheet of plastic on the paper. Rub the plastic for about a minute with the palm of your hand. Hold one corner of the plastic. Try to lift the plastic off the paper. What happens? Now pull the plastic and paper apart slowly. Can you hear the crackle of the electricity? When you rubbed the plastic, it became electrified.

FOLLOW UP:

    Use an electrified plastic sheet to pick up small pieces of paper. Use it to pick up pieces of thread. Stick it to the wall. Can you electrify a plastic comb or a plastic pen by rubbing it with wool? Can you electrify a wooden pencil?

HOW DOES ELECTRICITY TRAVEL?
(Electricity runs through wires)

YOU'LL NEED:

    dry cell   bulb
     2 thin wires (cut a small amount of insulation away from the ends)
    socket

HERE'S HOW:

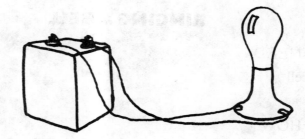

    A dry cell makes electricity. How can we send this electricity to a lamp? Wires will carry or conduct electricity. The lamp

133

holder is called a socket. Both the socket and the dry cell have two places to connect wires. When the wires are connected, does the lamp light?

TURNING ELECTRICITY ON AND OFF
(Switches start and stop the flow of electricity safely)

YOU'LL NEED:

dry cell   3 thin wires
bulb   socket
knife switch

HERE'S HOW:

Connect cell to lamp, lamp to switch, and switch to cell. The knife works like a little gate. What happens when you close the switch? You do not have to touch a wire while electricity is going through. In fact, don't do it because it is dangerous.

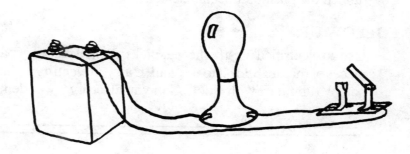

RINGING A BELL

YOU'LL NEED:

dry cell   3 thin wires
bell   buzzer

HERE'S HOW:

See if you can make the bell ring using the above materials. What makes the bell ring?

WHAT MATERIALS WILL CONDUCT ELECTRICITY?

A bulb will light when a metal is used to complete the circuit. Metals will conduct electric currents whereas nonmetals do not conduct electric current.

YOU'LL NEED:

      dry cell   3 covered wires (Scrape off the ends of each wire)
      several pieces of cloth, wood, glass, rubber, nails, pins, water, paper

HERE'S HOW:

      Connect cell to lamp, lamp to switch and switch to cell. (See Diagram A)

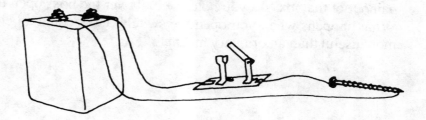

Throw the switch so that bulb lights. Open the circuit as shown in Diagram B for a place to test materials, but remove knife switch and include notation: "Place material here for testing."

Place a piece of cloth connecting the circuit and close the switch. Record whether or not the bulb lights. Do the same for the following materials: a) glass, b) wood, c) nail, d) pin, e) paper, and f) water. Record the results for each material.

MAKING AN ELECTROMAGNET
(Iron can be magnetized by electricity)

YOU'LL NEED:

    dry cell   knife switch
    large iron nail   few feet of covered bell wire

HERE'S HOW:

Scrape the covering off both ends of each wire. Wind the long wire around the nail, but leave the ends free. Make a circuit with the nail, but leave the ends free. Make a circuit with the nail and the open switch, as shown below. Dip the end of the nail into a box of pins and tacks. Close the knife switch and lift the nail out of the box. As you hold the nail over the box, open the knife switch. What happens when you open the switch? How could an electromagnet be more useful than an ordinary magnet?

Current Electricity
Activity Task Cards

task card #1

YOU'LL NEED:

    battery holder   bulb
    bulb socket   wire
    wire   clips

HERE'S HOW:

   Make this lightbulb work by making a closed circuit.

task card #2

YOU'LL NEED:

    circuit box   bulbs
    wire   clips
    batteries   holder

HERE'S HOW:

Get the circuit box from the science shelf. Use the objects to make a closed circuit. See if you light the bulb. Record your findings on "Report Paper" and place it in your science log. Or you may display your report on the bulletin board.

task card #3

YOU'LL NEED:

motor	bulb
socket	batter and holder
wire	colored art paper

HERE'S HOW:

Connect these objects to show a closed circuit. Make the motor run. Show an open circuit. Draw a picture about your evidence of interaction. Use colored art paper.

task card #4

YOU'LL NEED:

object box	wires
battery	bulb
socket	

HERE'S HOW:

Use objects for the "object box" to find out which objects are better conductors and which are better insulators. Place the objects that are conductors in the box. Place the objects that are insulators in the box top. Record your findings on a picture graph.

task card #5

YOU'LL NEED:

circuit puzzle box   electric circle puzzles
paper

HERE'S HOW:

Draw a line connecting the points that show a complete circuit on each card. Try it. Open them up to see if your choices were correct.

task card #6

YOU'LL NEED:

electric circuit puzzles   light bulbs
wires   batteries

HERE'S HOW:

Get the circuit puzzle box. Test puzzles to find connections that will close the circuit. Record on the paper in circuit puzzle box and place it in your science log.

task card #7

YOU'LL NEED:

dry cell

wires
paper

HERE'S HOW:

Fasten one end of each wire to a dry cell. Hold the wire by the covered parts. Touch two uncovered ends together. Tell about and draw what happened. Put a piece of paper between the two uncovered ends. What happens? Why?

task card #8

YOU'LL NEED:

wooden blocks
2 thumbtacks
copper wire

bulb
socket
dry cell

drawing paper

HERE'S HOW:

Make a switch with the first four objects. Next, use a dry cell. What happens? Do a picture story about it.

task card #9

YOU'LL NEED:

dry cell
motor

coper wire
tape recorder

HERE'S HOW:

Make this motor run. Record it on the tape recorder. What happened?

task card #10

YOU'LL NEED:

propeller
copper wires

dry cell

HERE'S HOW:

Make this propeller run. Use the dry cell and copper wires. Is this an open or closed circuit? Why? Record it in your log.

task card #11

YOU'LL NEED:

blue light bulb   brown socket
extension cord

HERE'S HOW:

Put the light bulb into an extension wire socket. What happens? Plug the extension cord into wall outlet. What happens? Take light bulb out of the extension cord. Put only half of the metal plug into the extension cord. Compare evidence of interaction. Record in log.

task card #12

YOU'LL NEED:

circuit board   dry cells
wires

HERE'S HOW:

How many different ways can you make a closed circuit on this board? How many circuits work?

task card # 13

YOU'LL NEED:

old lamp cord
crayons
tape or glue

scissors
construction paper

HERE'S HOW:

What is the purpose of insulation? What might happen without the insulation? Display the piece of cord and label the parts you see.

---

task card # 14

YOU'LL NEED:

little shoe box house
wire
socket

dry cell
bulb

HERE'S HOW:

Make the light bulb light the inside of the house. Make your own light house.

Static Electricity
Activity Task Cards

task card #1

YOU'LL NEED:

2 balloons
2 pieces of nylon thread (2 feet long)

piece of wool

HERE'S HOW:

Tie blown balloons to nylon threads, one balloon to each thread. Charge both balloons by rubbing them with wool. Hold the threads together.

THINK:

Can the balloons be brought together easily? Why? What happens when you bring your hand near the balloon? What happens when you bring your hand between the balloons? Record your observations on the report paper and in your science log.

task card #2

YOU'LL NEED:

2 balloons
plastic bag

piece of wool
2 pieces of nylon thread (2 feet long)

HERE'S HOW:

Tie blown balloons to nylon strings. Charge one balloon by rubbing it with the plastic bag. Hold the threads together.

THINK:

Do these balloons come together easily? Do they remain together? Why? Record your observations on report paper and in your science log.

task card #3

YOU'LL NEED:

        plastic box (no deeper than 1")   small, light objects
            (puffed rice, sawdust, small pieces of paper)
        piece of nylon or wool
            piece of aluminum foil to line the bottom of plastic box

HERE'S HOW:

Line the bottom of the plastic box with aluminum foil. Put some of the lightweight material into the box and close the cover. Rub the cover of the box with the wool or nylon. Watch what happens. Wrap up a dozen small pieces of puffed rice with small pieces of aluminum foil. Place them in the box and rub the cover. Record your observations on report paper and in log book.

task card #4

YOU'LL NEED:

        sheet of newspaper   plastic bag
        metal top from can

HERE'S HOW:

Rub the newspaper with the plastic bag for about fifteen seconds. Put the metal top in the center of the paper. Lift the paper off the table by lifting the edges of the paper.

THINK:

Ask someone to quickly move his or her fingers close to the metal top. What happens? Go to the material box and test out other materials in addition to the plastic bag. Which spark is the strongest? Why is this so? Write your observations on experiment report paper and in your science log.

task card #5

YOU'LL NEED:

    salt

    piece of wool

                                        pocket comb

HERE'S HOW:

Spill salt on the table. Charge a comb by rubbing it with wool, or by combing your hair briskly.

THINK:

What happens when this comb comes near the salt? What other materials could you use? How could you separate salt from pepper knowing what you know about static electricity? Record your observations on report paper and in your science log.

task card #6

YOU'LL NEED:

    plastic comb

    tiny pieces of paper

                                        piece of wool

HERE'S HOW:

Tear the paper into bits. Charge the comb with a piece of wool. What happens when the comb is brought close to the paper? Find some other things that would react the same way as the paper did. Record on experiment report paper and in your science log.

task card #7

YOU'LL NEED:

cotton thread (1' long)   nylon thread (1' long)
plastic comb   piece of wool

HERE'S HOW:

Charge the comb by rubbing it with wool. Bring the comb near the cotton thread.

THINK:

What happens? What difference, if any, is there when using nylon thread? Record your observations on report paper and in your science log.

task card #8

YOU'LL NEED:

pocket comb   ping pong ball
piece of wool

HERE'S HOW:

Place a ping pong ball on level table. Rub comb with wool to charge it.

THINK:

What happens when the charged comb is brought near the ping pong ball? What other materials from the material box will charge the comb? Record your observations on report paper and in your science log.

task card #9

YOU'LL NEED:

    2 strips of newspaper (1" wide x 20" high)
    plastic bag

HERE'S HOW:

Hold paper strips together, letting them hang straight down.

THINK:

What happens when you stroke them from top to bottom with your finger? What other materials can be stroked against the newspaper to make the same thing happen? What happens when more than two newspaper strips are used? Record your observations on report paper and in your science log.

task card #10

YOU'LL NEED:

    piece of newspaper (3" x 5")   scissors
    piece of plastic bag

HERE'S HOW:

Cut eight narrow strips down the 5" side of the newspaper. The strips should only be 3" long and should still be attached to the top of the paper. These strips will be the spider's legs. The top of the paper will be the spider's body.

THINK:

Hold the spider with its legs down against the wall. Rub it with a plastic for about ten strokes from top to bottom. What happens after a few strokes? Hold the spider by its body and lift it from the wall. What happens? Now hold your finger between the spider's legs. What happens? Record your observations on experiment report paper and in your science log.

148

task card #11

YOU'LL NEED:

   nylon stocking   plastic bag

HERE'S HOW:

   Hold stocking toe against wall. Rub stocking with plastic bag for about 10 strokes. Pull stocking from the wall.

THINK:

   What happens to the stocking? Why does this happen? Record your observations on experiment report paper and in your science log.

task card #12

YOU'LL NEED:

   playing cards   piece of rug

HERE'S HOW:

   Charge yourself by rubbing your feet on a carpet. See how many cards you can stick to the wall.

THINK:

   Does this work by rubbing the cards with other materials from the material box? How long will the cards stick to the wall? Record your observation on report paper and in your science log.

task card # 13

YOU'LL NEED:

wooden pencil   rug pieces

HERE'S HOW:

Balance the pencil on the back of a chair top so that it is free to move. Shuffle your feet on the rug. Hold your finger near the tip of the pencil. What does the pencil do? Try this using other charged objects. Record your observations on experiment report paper and in your science log.

task card # 14

YOU'LL NEED:

bottle with a cork   drinking straw
nylon thread   thumbtack
piece of rug

HERE'S HOW:

Cut off a piece of a straw that is smaller than the width of the bottle. Tie the thread tightly around the center of the straw. Attach the other end of the thread to the cork with a thumbtack. Drop the straw into the bottle, leaving it free to turn. Put the cork in the bottle. Rub your feet on the rug. Point your finger at the straw. What happens to the straw? Try this using other charged objects. Record your observations on experiment report paper and in science log.

task card #15

YOU'LL NEED:

a generator   drawing paper

HERE'S HOW:

Turn the handle slowly. What happens? Now, turn it quickly. What happens? Why? Draw a picture of it.

Related Electricity Activity Task Cards

task card #1

YOU'LL NEED:

    your imagination   pencil and paper

HERE'S HOW:

Start with the word "electricity" and make as many words that you can, extending from the letters. Example:

    b
    e
    l
    electricity
    a
    r
    d

task card #2

YOU'LL NEED:

    picture puzzle of electric appliance   art supplies

HERE'S HOW:

Put the puzzle pieces together. Make your own jugsaw puzzle.

task card #3

YOU'LL NEED:

Scrambled Word ditto *

HERE'S HOW:

The words on the Scrambled Word ditto have letters that are all mixed up. Try to unscramble them and discover each word. Check answer key for correct answers. Put completed ditto in your science log.

* Note to teacher: See Appendix A for Scrambled Word and Alphabetical Order dittos.

task card #4

YOU'LL NEED:

Alphabetical Order ditto *

HERE'S HOW:

Put the words on the Alphabetical Order ditto in their correct order. Check your answers on the answer key. Put completed ditto in your science log.

task card # 5

YOU'LL NEED:

    magazines   scissors

    glue   poster-graph

HERE'S HOW:

Get a group of five children together. Cut out pictures of electrical appliances from magazines and mount them in proper categories on the "Electricity Is Used in Many Ways" graph.

task card # 6

YOU'LL NEED:

    posterboard   art supplies

HERE'S HOW:

Create a safety poster. Show ways of avoiding an injury from any electrical appliance.

task card #7

YOU'LL NEED:

    construction paper   magazine pictures
    scissors   paste
    other art supplies

HERE'S HOW:

Write a poem about a battery. Display your poem on construction paper. Try making some background displays for your poem.

task card #8

YOU'LL NEED:

    construction paper   magazine pictures
    scissors   paste
    othert art supplies

HERE'S HOW:

Make a collage of magazine pictures to show the uses of electricity.

task card #9

YOU'LL NEED:

drawing paper   crayons or pencil

HERE'S HOW:

Look for switches in your home and school. Make pictures of all switches you can find.

task card #10

HERE'S HOW:

Choose some friends to play Electrical Appliance Charades with you. One person will act out the uses of an electrical appliance, without using any words to explain what he is doing. The other children will try to guess what the appliance is within one minute. Remember to keep an eye on the clock.

task card #11

HERE'S HOW:

Make up a T. V. commercial, trying to sell an electrical appliance. Draw a picture to go with it.

task card #12

HERE'S HOW:

Make up a play about Wanda Wire, Lenny Lightbulb, and Benny Battery. They all live in the Power House. Have fun! Be sure to write an invitation to the class to see your play.

task card #13

HERE'S HOW:

Play Electrical Appliance Charade (See Task Card #12). Keep track of how many times each player guesses a correct appliance. Make a graph to show outcome of the games.

task card #14

YOU'LL NEED:

hanger
pictures

string

HERE'S HOW:

Draw and/or find pictures of any object dealing with electricity. Cut them out. Punch a hole in the top of each object. Tie one end of a string through the hole and the other end to the hanger. Have each string cut to a different length. You've made a mobile!

task card #15

HERE'S HOW:

Get a friend or two and think of a familiar tune. Write new words for the song, all about electricity. After getting it all together and practicing it, sing your song for the whole class.

task card #16

YOU'LL NEED:

construction paper   white paper
pen

HERE'S HOW:

Make up an electricity picture-dictionary using many of the new words you have learned. Be sure your words are in alphabetical order.

task card # 17

YOU'LL NEED:

art materials   bulbs
wires   batteries

HERE'S HOW:

Get together with one or more classmates. Use an old shoe box to set up a popsicle stick puppet or finger puppet theatre. Be sure to use stage lights and sound effects. Make the puppets and write a short play. When the show is ready, be sure to invite the whole class to the opening performance.

task card # 18

HERE'S HOW:

Imagine you are a light bulb. Write a story about "A Day in the Life of Light Bulb" on picture story paper. Display your story and share it with your classmates.

task card #19

YOU'LL NEED:

   materials from resource table

HERE'S HOW:

   Do a little research to find out why electricity makes the light bulb light up. (Hint: The word *resistance* is important) Write a paragraph on your findings. Put it in your science log. Be sure to use good paragraph form and proper punctuation.

task card #20

YOU'LL NEED:

   materials from resource table

HERE'S HOW:

   Who is Thomas A. Edison and what contributions did he make? Write the information on paper and put it in your science log.

task card #21

HERE'S HOW:

Read a book about Thomas Edison or Ben Franklin. Write a short biography about the man you choose. Keep it in your science log or display it, after having it checked.

task card #22

HERE'S HOW:

Write a short poem about "I Wish I Were a..." (light bulb, battery, circuit, wire, radio, balloon, or light switch). Draw a picture.

task card #23

HERE'S HOW:

Make believe you are an electrical appliance. Draw a picture of yourself at work. Write an interesting story about yourself.

task card #24

HERE'S HOW:

A new (make-believe) law has been passed that each home will be allowed only one electrical object. Which would you choose? Write about your reasons for choosing this object.

task card # 25

HERE'S HOW:

Write a letter to your electrical company. Invite them to send a speaker to discuss safe ways of using electricity.

task card # 26

HERE'S HOW:

Write a "What if" story. What if . . .

There were no traffic lights?

There were no lightbulbs?

There was a blackout?

Every time you touched a person he turned into a light bulb, or a battery, or a wire?

task card #27

HERE'S HOW:

Talk to the school custodian and find out how a fuse works. Record the information in your science log.

task card #28

HERE'S HOW:

What did people do in Colonial times before electricity was discovered? Use your science log to record your researched information.

task card #29

Ch. IX

HERE'S HOW:

Write a story about:

Baby Wire Goes to Circuit Land

The Adventures of Benny Battery

task card #30

Ch. IX

HERE'S HOW:

Make a list of safety rules to follow when you use electricity.

task card #31

YOU'LL NEED:
Number Problems ditto *

HERE'S HOW:
Complete number problems. Check the code to discover mystery word. Check your answers on the answer key. File the ditto in your science log.

task card #32

YOU'LL NEED:
Crossword Puzzle ditto *

HERE'S HOW:
Complete crossword puzzle by filling in the appropriate spaces with the correct answers. Check the answer key for the correct answers. File the ditto in your science log.

* Note to teachers: See Appendix A for Crossword Puzzle ditto.

Resources

Adler, Irving. *Electricity in Your Life*. New York: John Day Co., 1965.

Corbett, Scott. *What Makes a Light Go On?* Boston, Mass.: Little, Brown and Co., 1966.

Epstein, Sam and Beryl. *The First Book of Electricity*. New York: Franklin Watts, 1953.

Feravolo, Rocco V. *Junior Science Book of Electricity*. Champaign, Ill.: Garrard Publishing Co., 1960.

Frasier, George, et. al. *Singer Science All the Year*. Syracuse, New York: The L. W. Singer Co., Inc., 1959.

_____. *Fun with Science*. New York: Scholastic Book Services, 1968.

Freeman, Ira. *All About Electricity*. New York: Random House, 1957.

Freeman, Mae and Ira Freeman. *The Story of Electricity*. Eau Claire, Wis.: E.M. Hale and Co., 1961.

Graf, Rudolf. *Safe and Simple Electrical Experiments*. New York: Dover Publications, Inc., 1964.

Guthridge, Sue. *Tom Edison: Boy Inventor*. New York: Bobbs Merrill, Co., Inc., 1959.

Kerner, Ben. *Electricity*. New York: Coward-McCann, Inc., 1965.

North, Sterling. *Young Thomas Edison*. Boston, Mass.: Houghton Mifflin, 1958.

Parker, Berta Morris. *Electricity*. Evanston, Ill., Row, Peterson and Co., 1960.

Pine, Tillie and Joseph Levine. *Electricity and How to Use It*. New York: Whittlesey House, 1962.

Podendorf, Illa. *Magnets and Electricity*. Chicago, Ill.: Children's Press, 1961.

Rosenfeld, Sam. *The Magic of Electricity*. New York: Young Reader's Press, 1963.

Shepherd, Walter. *Electricity*. New York: John Day Co., 1964.

Scarf, Maggi. *Meet Benjamin Franklin*. New York: Random House, 1968.

Schneider, Herman and Nina. *More Power to You*. New York: William Scott, Inc., 1953.

_____. *Science Fun with Milk Cartons*. New York: McGraw, Hill Book Co., 1963.

_____. *Science for Here and Now*. Boston, Mass.: D.C. Heath and Co., 1961.

_____. *Science in Your Life*. Boston, Mass.: D.C. Heath and Co., 1961.

_____. *Science in Our World*. Boston, Mass.: D.C. Heath and Co., 1961.

Shapp, Martha and Charles. *Let's Find Out About Thomas Alva Edison*. New York: Franklin Watt, Inc., 1966.

Swezey, Kenneth. *Science Shows You How*. New York: McGraw, Hill Book Co., 1964.

Syrocki, B. John. *What is Electricity*. Chicago, Ill.: Benefic Press, 1960.

Wyler, Rose. *The First Book of Science Experiments*. New York: Franklin Watt, Inc., 1952.

Films

Electricity and How It's Made.
Making Electricity.

Filmstrips

Electricity All Around Us. Budek Films and Slides, Inc., 1968.
Experimenting with Static Electricity. Encyclopedia Britannica, 1968.
Making Electricity. Popular Science Publishing Co., 1961.
Simple Electrical Circuits. Popular Science Publishing Co., 1969.
Static Electricity. Popular Science Publishing Co., 1964.

Appendix A

Dittos for Related Electricity Activity Task Cards & Answer Key

Unscramble these words:

Use Answer Key # 1

1) r r e u n c t _____.
2) b l i t g l b u h _____.
3) t n f i i r c o _____.
4) g e r y n e _____.
5) c t w s i h _____.
6) u t r o c c d n o _____.
7) t i c t e l c e r y i _____.
8) l e c d y l r _____.
9) m t g i a l n e _____.
10) t i c r u i c _____.
11) e w p o t _____.
12) e y t b t a r _____.
13) t s a i c t _____.
14) t s a i c t _____.
15) g u p l _____.

Put these words in alphabetical order:

Use Answer Key # 2

_____ electricity

_____ current

_____ motor

_____ power

_____ battery

_____ light bulb

_____ static

_____ flashlight

_____ plug

_____ switch

_____ conductor

_____ fuse

_____ dry cell

_____ filament

_____ circuit

_____ friction

_____ energy

_____ wire

_____ outlet

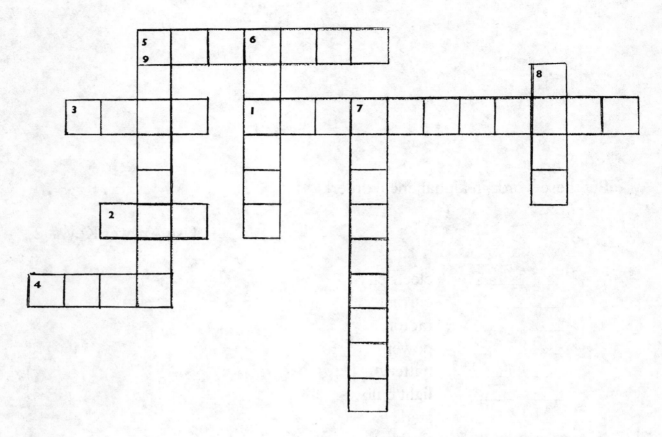

Use Answer Key # 3

Across

1) refrigerators run by _____.
2) A long snake-like animal.
3) The lamp wouldn't work because the _____ burned out.
4) A radiator makes _____.
5) You put fuses in a _____.

Down

6) Because of shortages in fuel, we have an _____ crisis.
7) This group of objects lets electricity travel through them easily.
8) Ben Franklin hung a key from his _____ string.
9) The _____ inside a lightbulb is what lights up.

174

ANSWER KEYS

Answer Key #1 (Task Card #3 — Scrambled Words)

1) current
2) lightbulb
3) friction
4) energy
5) switch
6) conductor
7) electricity
8) dry cell
9) filament
10) circuit
11) power
12) battery
13) static
14) plug

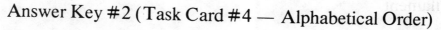

Answer Key #2 (Task Card #4 — Alphabetical Order)

1) battery
2) circuit
3) conductor
4) current
5) dry cell
6) electricity
7) energy
8) filament
9) flashlight
10) friction
11) fuse
12) light bulb
13) motor
14) outlet
15) plug
16) power
17) static
18) switch
19) wire

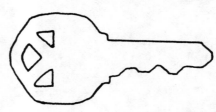

Answer Key #3 (Task Card #32 — Crossword Puzzle)

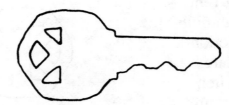

Across

1) electricity
2) eel
3) bulb
4) heat
5) fusebox

Down

6) energy
7) conductor
8) kite
9) filament

Appendix B

Teacher Aids
&
Resources

LOOK AT ME!

I am . . .

a noisy worker _____ a quiet worker

a neat worker _____ a messy worker

able to work by myself _____ always asking for help

usually able
to finish my work _____
usually unable
to finish my work

- CONTRACT -

_____(Student)_____   with   _____(Teacher)_____

_____(date)_____

Subject: _____

Contractual Conditions

What I want to find out:	**How I will show what I learned:**
_____	_____
_____	_____
_____	_____
_____	_____
_____	_____
_____	_____
_____	_____
_____	_____

Due Date: _____

Consequences: _____
_____
_____
_____
_____

LOG OF MY INDEPENDENT STUDY

Date	Accomplishments	Evaluation	Next Step (Plans)

INDEPENDENT STUDY PROFILE

Name: _____ **Subject:** _____ **Date:** _____

Directions: Place a check on each continuum to show how you feel about the independent study you have completed.

1) USE OF RESOURCES:

many _____ few

same _____ different

2) FINISHED PROJECT (OR PRODUCT) :

ordinary _____ unlike any others

written _____ constructed

3) USE OF TIME:

wasted _____ worked hard

4) FEELINGS ABOUT THE STUDY:

satisfied _____ dissatisfied

learned enough _____ need to learn more

The Successful Teacher's Most Valuable Resource!

EDUCATION

THE EARLI PROGRAM
Excellent language development program! Volume I contains developmentally sequenced lessons in verbal receptive language; Volume II, expressive language. Use as a primary, supplemental or rehabilitative language program.

| Volume I | No. 067-7 | $14.95 |
| Volume II | No. 074-X | $14.95 |

LEARNING ENVIRONMENTS FOR CHILDREN
A practical manual for creating efficient, pleasant and stress-free learning environments for children centers. Make the best possible use of your center's space!

No. 065-0 $12.95

COMPETENCIES:
A Self-Study Guide to Teaching Competencies in Early Childhood Education
This comprehensive guide is ideal for evaluating or improving your competency in early childhood education or preparing for the CDA credential.

No. 024-3 $12.95

LOOKING AT CHILDREN:
Field Experiences in Child Study
A series of fourteen units made up of structured exercises dealing with such issues as language development, play and moral development in children. A fresh new approach to learning materials for early childhood educators.

No. 001-4 $12.95

YOUNG CHILDREN'S BEHAVIOR:
Implementing Your Goals
A variety of up-to-date approaches to discipline and guidance to help you deal more effectively with children. Also an excellent addition to CDA and competency-based training programs.

No. 015-4 $7.95

NUTS AND BOLTS
The ultimate guide to classroom organization and management of an early learning environment. Provides complete guidelines for setting up an early learning center; also excellent for improving an existing school system.

No. 063-4 $6.95

READING ROOTS:
Teach Your Child
Teach your child a basic reading vocabulary centered around the colors of his crayons before he enters school. Enjoyable coloring and matching activities make learning to read fun for both you and your child.

No. 070-7 $10.95

BACK TO BASICS IN READING MADE FUN
Refreshing and innovative approach to teaching basic reading skills which will delight and stimulate students. Over 100 creative games and projects to use in designing exciting reading materials.

No. 060-X $12.95

ACTIVITY BOOKS

EARLY CHILDHOOD ACTIVITIES:
A Treasury of Ideas from Worldwide Sources
A virtual encyclopedia of projects, games and activities for children aged 3 to 7, containing over 500 different child-tested activities drawn from a variety of teaching systems. The ultimate activity book!

No. 066-9 $16.95

VANILLA MANILA FOLDER GAMES
Make exciting and stimulating Vanilla Manila Folder Games quickly and easily with simple manila file folders and colored marking pens. Unique learning activities designed for children aged 3 to 8.

No. 059-6 $14.95

HANDBOOK OF LEARNING ACTIVITIES
Over 125 exciting, enjoyable activities and projects for young children in the areas of math, health and safety, play, movement, science, social studies, art, language development, puppetry and more!

No. 058-8 $14.95

MONTH BY MONTH ACTIVITY GUIDE FOR THE PRIMARY GRADES
Month by Month gives you a succinct guide to the effective recruitment and utilization of teachers' aides plus a full year's worth of fun-filled educational activities in such areas as reading, math, art, and science.

No. 061-8 $14.95

ART PROJECTS FOR YOUNG CHILDREN
Build a basic art program of stimulating projects on a limited budget and time schedule with Art Projects. Contains over 100 fun-filled projects in the areas of drawing, painting, puppets, clay, printing and more!

No. 051-0 $12.95

AEROSPACE PROJECTS FOR YOUNG CHILDREN
Introduce children to the fascinating field of aerospace with the exciting and informative projects and field trip suggestions. Contributors include over 30 aviation/aerospace agencies and personnel.

No. 052-9 $12.95

CHILD'S PLAY:
An Activities and Materials Handbook
An eclectic selection of fun-filled activities for preschool children designed to lend excitement to the learning process. Activities include puppets, mobiles, poetry, songs and more.

No. 003-0 $12.95

ENERGY:
A Curriculum for 3, 4 and 5 Year Olds
Help preschool children become aware of what energy is, the sources of energy, the uses of energy and wise energy use with the fun-filled activities, songs and games included in this innovative manual.

No. 069-3 $9.95

HUMANICS LIMITED

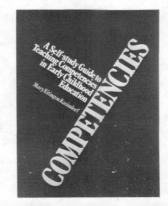

ORDER FORM

HUMANICS LIMITED
P.O. BOX 7447/Atlanta, Georgia 30309

FOR FAST SERVICE
CALL COLLECT (404) 874-2176

QUANTITY ORDERED	ORDER NO.	BOOK TITLE	UNIT PRICE	TOTAL PRICE

☐ Payment Enclosed

☐ Institutional Purchase Order No. _____

☐ Bill my Credit Card

WHEN USING A CREDIT CARD, PLEASE CHECK PROPER BOX AND GIVE APPROPRIATE CARD AND NUMBER INFORMATION.

☐ MASTER CARD   ☐ VISA

Credit Card No.
Master Card Interbank No.
Exp. Date month/year

Authorized Signature (Order must be signed)

PLEASE TYPE, OR PRINT CLEARLY.

Subtotal	
Georgia residents add 5% sales tax	
Add shipping and handling charges	
TOTAL ORDER	

SHIP TO:

NAME
ADDRESS
CITY/STATE _____ ZIP
TELEPHONE ( )

Shipping and Handling Charges

Up to $10.00 add	$1.60
$10.01 to $20.00 add	$2.60
$20.01 to $40.00 add	$3.60
$40.01 to $70.00 add	$4.60
$70.01 to $100.00 add	$5.60
$100.01 to $125.00 add	$6.60
$125.01 to $150.00 add	$7.60
$150.01 to $175.00 add	$8.60
$175.01 to $200.00 add	$9.60

Orders over $200 vary depending on method of shipment.